Dear Sis,
Not just...
Not just a friend —
but a sister &

...but, I CAN'T FORGIVE MYSELF

Love,
Lana Sanders
May 24, 2017

LANA SANDERS

...but, I CAN'T FORGIVE MYSELF

AN UNNECESSARY BURDEN

TATE PUBLISHING
AND ENTERPRISES, LLC

...*But, I Can't Forgive Myself*
Copyright © 2014 by Lana Sanders. All rights reserved.

No part of this publication may be reproduced, stored in a retrieval system or transmitted in any way by any means, electronic, mechanical, photocopy, recording or otherwise without the prior permission of the author except as provided by USA copyright law.

The opinions expressed by the author are not necessarily those of Tate Publishing, LLC.

Published by Tate Publishing & Enterprises, LLC
127 E. Trade Center Terrace | Mustang, Oklahoma 73064 USA
1.888.361.9473 | www.tatepublishing.com

Tate Publishing is committed to excellence in the publishing industry. The company reflects the philosophy established by the founders, based on Psalm 68:11,
"The Lord gave the word and great was the company of those who published it."

Book design copyright © 2014 by Tate Publishing, LLC. All rights reserved.
Cover design by Junriel Boquecosa
Interior design by Mary Jean Archival

Published in the United States of America

ISBN: 978-1-63185-431-6
Religion / Christian Life / Social Issues
14.04.14

This book is dedicated to the brave, brokenhearted women and men who have been healed in this ministry, Beauty for Ashes Ministries International, from 1992 to date, 2014. One of the common struggles of these women and men has been the quest to forgive themselves. I have been blessed by God to walk with them through their journey to healing, and I pray that multitudes of men and women will find freedom in the truth found in the pages of *But I Can't Forgive Myself!*

ACKNOWLEDGMENTS

My heart cheers my precious husband for his faithful support in ministry for the past thirty plus years. We are, always have been, and always will be partners in God's calling on our lives. God called us both to full-time service in his kingdom, and thankfully at the same time. I am so grateful for the way we have grown in Christ together. We have learned and lived the equation: 1+1+1=1; God plus Ray plus me equals one. Ray is my greatest cheerleader, most steadfast supporter, trustworthy confidant, optimistic visionary, and godly covering in all God calls us to do in ministry. Ray is my rock star, for he is a rock-steady man of God, no less steady than the Rock of Gibraltar. Without him, I would have struggled far more and accomplished far less for God's kingdom. Darling, I love you eternally!

With extreme gratitude, we acknowledge John and Debbie Fox for their 2013 donation, making the publication of this book possible.

I am so thankful for my pastor's support and friendship. Jana Meeks, a pastor and pastor's wife is one of the most amazing daughters of the King of kings I've known. She is a spiritual covering, but most of all, she is my sweet sister in Christ and close friend. She has walked with me and prayed me through great testing and glorious victories. I would be a bit lost without her. Thank you, Jana!

My heartfelt gratitude to those whose eyes looked tirelessly for mistakes in this manuscript, especially Sheray Morrison and Linda Demjen.

God's family is among our greatest blessings! God placed Ray and I in a church home where we could walk with His children in His house and through our lives as we learn godly integrity and unconditional love. As humans, it is impossible to love like God loves, with *agape* (unconditional love). Lindale Church has been truly home to us, and His children there have been our true and faithful family of choice. We have many brothers and sisters in Christ who worship at other churches, and we love and treasure each one. Friends, Ray and I love you all deeply and thank God for you!

Thank you, Abba, for Your trust to preach, to teach, and to write about Your holy Word! *Wow*, Lord, what a privilege, great responsibility, unspeakable joy, and humbling call. Ray and I thank You for calling us to and keeping us in this powerful ministry.

CONTENTS

Introduction 11
Prologue 17
Devastated 19
One of the Worst Days of My Life 31
Being Forgiven 35
An Unnecessary Burden 49
Forgiveness Two Ways 55
God Requires Us to Forgive! 83
"But I Can't Forgive Myself" 93
Staying Free 101
Our Son 103
Messengers 109
A Major Test! 115
The Ripple Effect 119
Holy Blood 123
Epilogue 129
About the Author 131
Notes 133

INTRODUCTION

"I know God has forgiven me… but I can't forgive myself." This is a statement I've made at times, and I've heard it repeated countless times.

Before my loved ones and friends read this book and wonder why I exposed some aspects of my previous life of sin, let me say, I do so in the shadow of the Cross. God asked me to write this book in a way that others can relate to the transformation that God's love and grace can make in a life so they will have hope. He also wants a much overlooked and liberating truth to set His people free and lead the lost to Him. I did not enjoy writing about my former life, which was away from God, but it was necessary to obey my Lord. I will say there is no pain left in those memories. God has truly healed my heart to the uttermost, so the testimony of my life becomes His testimony. As you read, I hope you think of the sinful women in the Bible who were transformed by God's grace and then used for His glory!

My life was devastated by choices. Since my earliest memory, others made choices that wounded my very being:

sexual abuse, abandonment, divorce, and loss of all that was precious to me. If that was not bad enough, my resulting choices were the most harmful. My life became a dark and desperate attempt at self-protection while becoming self-destructive. The nightlife of Houston, Texas became my reality, and I seldom saw the light of day. The darkness in my life grew in intensity until I was swallowed by it. Everywhere I went and worked and played was densely dark. I know now I was hiding in this darkness, but for twelve years, it was a way of life for me.

In this darkness, trust was impossible, and clear vision was eliminated. Most of the night clubs I worked in were only lit by little red table top candles. Each table had its own limited amount of light, and the next table was barely visible. Shame is comfortable in darkness, and I was filled with it. Guilt is numbed by darkness, and I was eaten up with it.

There were many strip clubs in Houston, but by God's grace, that was not what drew me. I was drawn to the night clubs and all the money I could make working there. The money was a lure, but darkness to hide my shame was the hook that caught me. Money and all the sin it took to get it was my passion. Many men were used and discarded by my quest to get more. I would discard them before they had a chance to do the same to me. Then one day, all that changed.

On one sunny afternoon, the door to the dark club where I worked opened and a tall man stood as a silhouette in the doorway. All I could see was his six-feet-two-inch frame, but somehow knew I wanted to meet him. This was very unusual for me. I had a self-rule that I never dated customers for I was in management and would not allow my waitresses to date their customers. The purpose of the rule was so our tips would not decrease. This was in the seventies and it was not unusual for me to make several hundred dollars a night. That was a lot of money in that decade. The thing was I owned nothing but a lot of pretty clothes and shoes to show for it. The irony was I only wore them in darkness!

This afternoon was different, and I made it a point to attract this man standing in the doorway. That evening was our first dance and date. He proposed two weeks later, and I accepted. It took a trip around the world to hook him into marriage in 1978. I will tell you more about that later.

Before Ray came into my life, I had been married and divorced twice, and though I felt I needed men, I really hated them. Every man in my early life had hurt me. Since my first divorce, I had set about to return that hurt to every man who gave me a chance. I would charm and seduce them with the plan to get all I could from them and then hurt them in some way. The confusing, sad thing was I so wanted to be loved all this time but was afraid. Fear is a powerful motivator!

Fast-forward with me to one day in early 1991 when my third husband and I applied to volunteer at a Crisis Pregnancy Center in Houston, Texas. We did so before we really knew what a pregnancy center was or what they did. We only knew they were doing something about abortion and we were not. This was a problem for us because we had fallen in love with Jesus ten years before, and our hearts belonged to Him.

About that time in 1991, people had begun to talk about abortion and the after effects, and we began to realize how God felt about it. This mattered to us because Ray and I both chose abortions before we met. I had two, and he had one. You may think, "But he's a man and couldn't have an abortion." The truth is every aborted baby has a father and many carry a heavy load of guilt and shame from an abortion they forced, agreed to, or influenced. Also, many men have a broken heart because they did not want their baby aborted but couldn't prevent it. What Ray and I did not realize is how our abortions had affected our lives, much less how it had broken our hearts. So when we went to see a Christian theatrical drama, not knowing it was about abortion and the emotional after effects, we could not leave before getting involved in some way, so we volunteered at a local crisis pregnancy center.

Of course, we were convinced we were really all right. By this time, we were respected leaders in our church, and while convincing others we were okay, we convinced ourselves. We were what we now call Mr. and Mrs. Lookright. No one would have guessed we needed healing and never would anyone have guessed we had abortions in our past! It was certainly true that we had been transformed in numerous ways by sitting under the Word of God for ten years, and we had both been healed of so much heartache. The truth we did not want to face was there was pain buried deep in both our hearts. Abortion was not all we carried shame and guilt for. Those tragic choices were preceded and followed by a lifestyle of sin and pain.

God knew the pain we carried! He would not leave us as broken servants. He wanted to completely heal and restore His children. So long before we knew what we most desperately needed, our Father in heaven began to work His plan to restore us.

Ray accepted Jesus in 1981, and I rededicated my life to Christ the same day. In 1991 God began our healing from the deepest and darkest secret pain. Jesus' sacrificial death on the cross was for our total restoration, and we could go nowhere else to receive what our broken hearts needed. We hope you will begin your journey to complete restoration as you read this little book, no matter what has broken your heart.

PROLOGUE

There was a little girl, not an only child but a child rejected and abused, who at the tender age of only four found refuge in climbing a tree, spending hours of the day. This little girl did not realize until later in life she had been rejected from the womb. Born into a dysfunctional family, as the youngest of four children in the post-WWII years, news of her conception was an unexpected burden to her mother. This child, with an alcoholic father suffering from post-traumatic stress disorder (PTSD) and an ill mother with a broken heart, trusted far too many who could not be trusted with her innocence.

She had a faith in God beyond her years and fearlessly accepted Jesus as her personal Savior at five in a small church in north Houston, Texas. She loved and knew Jesus for real and was called to ministry immediately after making Christ her Savior. At playtime, before she was in preschool, she would pretend she was a preacher of the gospel and grew to fulfill that calling as an adult, but tragically not until after many years of abuse and personal sin. She did not realize how unhappy she was at home until she was in the seventh grade of school, at which time she left home. Turn the pages of this book to get to know her better and to learn a liberating truth, which could help you live free in the love of God.

DEVASTATED

I met my husband, of now thirty-five years, in 1978 when I was like Humpty Dumpty. My heart was broken in so many places that no one on earth could put me back together again. I had previously been married to my son's father for seven years, divorced, and married briefly again for eight months, then single for nine years. I was unaware God was about to bring such a wonderful man into my life. Ray came into my life when my heart was broken in a million pieces. My heart had hardened and the pieces looked like they were together, but my heart was fragile and fractured.

Into my chaos walked a tall, handsome, sweet man. I had been through a personal process of elimination of men by being very sexually promiscuous and living in an emotional vacuum. Ray had no idea what he was getting into. Without my knowledge, the miraculous was taking place as God planned to put His kind of love in this man for me. I felt so unworthy of love, and I sabotaged our relationship almost every day for the first three years. Anger had produced a root of bitterness in my heart, and it was contaminating my marriage.

> Looking carefully lest anyone fall short of the grace of God; lest any root of bitterness springing up cause trouble, and by this many become defiled. (Hebrews 12:15, NKJV)

One of my greatest struggles was in believing such a great guy could really love me. This insecurity manifested in rages of jealousy. I was either jealous or I would just refuse to believe Ray really loved me. I was so damaged that I could not accept true love. The amazing thing is, a person can look like they have it altogether and be broken beyond repair. I looked like I was in control of my life when really anger was in control.

Go back with me for a few minutes to a front yard in North Houston, in the early 1950s, where the youngest of four children played outside all day and didn't realize how her pretend world would soon change in a very real way. A tallow tree in that front yard was the safest place in her world, so she climbed it every day and stayed there most of the day. She would take her doll and color book and sit on a limb leaning against the tree trunk and daydream. My perspective seemed clear from that lofty position. At least it was as clear as a four-year-old can imagine.

Being the youngest of four children, I adored my daddy. He was tall and so handsome. He was talented, and it seemed he could do anything, anything but quit drinking alcohol. He came home from WWII injured and addicted to alcohol. As far as I know, post-traumatic stress disorder had not been discovered at that time. I now know PTSD was exactly what my daddy suffered.

My two brothers were my mother's pride and my sister was her joy. My mother struggled to feed her three children with an out-of-work, alcoholic husband and she was not expecting another child when I was conceived. Doverside Baptist Church on Berry Road in North Houston and a next-door neighbor fed us most of the time. The neighbor owned a produce truck, and we often had vegetables and fruit from him. My mother was physically ill with severe anemia and a broken heart from a failing marriage and alcoholic husband whom she loved so much. Many times my daddy would walk for a loaf of bread and disappear for weeks at a time, only to show up again when his military disability check was due. In this setting, my mother became pregnant with me. From the beginning of my conception, I was an unwanted burden. I understand so clearly now, but for most of my life, it just felt like rejection, and it hurt.

As children, we often heard the name Johnny Black who owned a beer joint my daddy practically lived at. I hated Johnny Black's bar! It wasn't until my daddy's death, when I was twenty-one, that I learned Johnny was my daddy's illegitimate son. He came to the funeral, and I asked him. Somehow, I was both angry at Johnny while being somehow comforted that at least our daddy didn't choose a stranger over us.

Our mother adored our daddy in spite of his drinking and stuck it out with him until my eldest brother was fifteen and I was five. When she left our daddy, we moved from the house we knew, and she became even more ill and indigent. My two brothers went to Boy's Harbor, a home for destitute boys in La Porte, Texas and my sister and I stayed with our mother. I don't know what the compelling reason was for the decision to send our brothers away, but I know it changed both my brother's lives in a negative way, especially for my eldest brother. His anger was later unleashed on both my sister and me.

We lived with our mother in the back of a big house where there were insurance offices. My mother cleaned the offices daily for the rent, and my sister went to elementary school. I spent my days in a pretend world. There was no tree to climb there, so most often I pretended I was a preacher as I played on the big front porch in front of the insurance offices. There was no front yard, and I would preach to the shells in the street from the porch. In my imagination, they had faces. Seeing them as imaginary people, I told them everything I knew about Jesus, Moses, Jonah and the whale, Zacchaeus the wee little man, and others. I would lead the singing and take up the offering. Little did I know the plans God had for me! God told Jeremiah, "For I know the thoughts I have of you, says the LORD, thoughts of peace and not of evil, to give you a future and a hope" (Jeremiah 29:11, NKJV). God also told Jeremiah that before he was in his mother's womb, He knew him and called him (Jeremiah 5:1).

During this period, my aunt and uncle lived around the corner and took us to church. The same church is my home church now, all these years later. It was there I learned about Jesus as a child and loved Him with all of my little heart.

At some point in this time frame, I began to search for a father figure. This search made me vulnerable to men in my family as I looked for a protective hero. In the absence of my daddy's protection as well as my two older brothers' absence, several men in our family sexually abused me. However, my first abuser was my eldest brother while he was on a home visit from Boy's Harbor. He was one of my first and foremost heroes, and I adored him! A year later, he joined the air force at seventeen and became very violent as an air police, receiving a dishonorable discharge for beating a man. His childhood anger was beginning to manifest in violence. He returned home married to a woman with a small son. My brother's relationship with me was controlling and manipulative for years to come.

The first abuse by my brother was followed by uncles and a cousin sexually abusing me. My innocent pretend world was darkened by this unanswered question: Why did every hero I trusted use and abuse me in the same nasty way? Sexual predators always tell a child something to keep their victim from telling. Because it is an adult's warning to a child, it is extremely effective. I don't remember what these abusers told me, but I remember believing it must all be my fault.

Accepting Jesus as my personal Savior at age five, I earnestly gave my life to Him. The innocence He gave me was confused by the innocence men took from me. Now I realize from the moment of the first abuse, I began to hide shame deep in my heart, and only God knew about it.

There were other abusers as girlfriend's fathers would sneak in the bedroom when I would spend the night in their home, and again, I would be abused sexually. Then there was a trusted elderly man at church, a stranger on the beach, and other faceless men who took what they wanted from a little girl who just wanted a daddy. Little girls who do not know whom to trust do not tell anyone. I was grown with a child before I told my mother. Her reply came from her childhood abuse and the need to justify it. She said, "Oh that happens to every little girl. It happened to me, just get over it." I do not know if my mother ever allowed God to heal her broken heart before she went to heaven. I hope so! To this day, I recoil when I hear, "Just get over it." Some things are very hard to recover from, and that statement never helps.

My sister and I grew up to be very unhappy at home. Our mother had remarried when I was eight. When they married, we moved from behind the insurance offices to a modest home, and my mother went to work. She was a master seamstress and worked very hard to create beautiful clothing and home décor. My stepfather was a decent man who did not drink alcohol but rarely spoke to us. He really had no idea how to be a daddy or how to relate to children. Our home seemed safe, but we still did not have the daddy we needed so much. We both just wanted to be loved, and at a far too early age, we wanted our own home. Our mother loved Jesus, but after she married, she stopped going to church with us; and my sister and I would walk to the closest church or ride with someone to their church. That changed our family dynamic in ways we would not realize until much later.

My sister Glenda married young. She was three years older than me, and at sixteen, she married a twenty-three-year-old man she did not truly love. He was her best friend's brother and an ex-marine. He was her way out. This part of our history was ironically the same. Shorty after she married, I left home at thirteen, moved in with her and her husband and their premature baby boy.

My sister and her husband did not go to church so I stopped too. Jesus was not part of my life for those three years until I left their home. I moved in with an aunt and uncle who took me to church, and so I was back at my childhood church. I had fallen in love with a man who I met before I left my sister's home. I was only at my aunt's for a few months before he came back to Houston and into my life.

Again, I followed in my sister's footsteps to marry a man of twenty-three when I was still sixteen. I will say I did love him and the dream of marriage and my own home. I moved to a town in West Texas and married in his parents' living room. My sister, pregnant with her second child, moved with her husband and son to Odessa at that same time. Glenda was miserable there, and I was caught up in a fairy tale life, which seemed perfect. I felt like I was a princess in this new family. Finally, I had the family I had dreamed of as a child. My husband was the only son of an only son, and they had a very comfortable life of prosperity. Every little girl's fantasy is to be Cinderella, and I was about to become such a princess. My husband's father treated me like the daughter he always wanted. He was a very selfish man, but I couldn't see that then. His mother loved me as I had always wanted to be loved by a mother, and I adored her.

Marrying a nonbeliever, I walked away from my Savior, again. My new family seemed so perfect, and God was not part of their perfect life. My husband and his father and mother were not even acquainted with Christ. I was now the princess of the family. They idolized and possessed me. For the first few years, this was like a fairy tale to me and a dream come true. It became apparent after a few years that my marriage was more like a prison than a fairy tale. These were decent people, but looking back, I know their love was not God's kind of love.

We had a miscarriage when I was seventeen, and a few months after I turned eighteen I gave birth to a beautiful baby boy. The pregnancy was difficult with me being confined to bed for seven of the nine months. Our baby boy was a miracle. We loved each other, and we adored our son, but our marriage came unraveled after almost seven years because Jesus was not the center of our lives.

There were weeks at a time when I was not allowed to leave the house for my husband's fear that something would happen to me. He would often follow an ambulance to the only hospital fearing I was in it. Afterward, I was not allowed to leave home for days at a time. It was extremely smothering for a fearless young bride who had always been a people person and loved everyone. Remember, I even made friends of the shells in the street so I would have someone to talk to. Now, a young wife and mother, I was only allowed to be with my mother-in-law's friends where we would sit at one of their kitchen tables all day and play Yahtzee. My mother-in-law had always wanted a daughter, and she treated me like I was her own. Still, she and her friends were not my age, and I wanted that so much.

I tried to be the perfect wife, homemaker, and mother. I cleaned house with a vengeance and cooked three meals a day with passion. I would bake bread for breakfast, lunch, and dinner. I was so proud of myself, and though we lived in town, I felt like a farmer's wife. My husband was nothing like a farmer but loved anything that kept me home. I could not do enough to fill my loneliness. I missed people, and though I did not realize it, I missed Jesus!

I remember my twenty-first birthday. We celebrated it in our backyard with my new parents and no friends. Everyone drank but me. It was such a disappointment. I don't know what I imagined a twenty-first birthday to be, but it was not that. After five years of being lonely for people, I began to work in direct sales. I sold women's products at age twenty-one against my husband's protests. We never had friends. He had only a few friends, and he did not want me to have many either. He wanted our world to stay very small and often told me that our baby and I was all he wanted.

I had developed severe breast pains after my son was born, and my doctor recommended a certain undergarment that was only available by direct sales. It helped my condition so much I was sold on it and wanted others to know what a fabulous product it was! There were other products for women, and they were all exceptional and very easy to sell. I was primed for direct sales, and a new world opened up for me. I excelled in this new business in record time. A little at a time, I began to stay out longer than a sales party required to have a little fun with a girlfriend I had met through the new multilevel business. This enraged my husband, but I had gone from trying my best to please him to not caring if he was angry at me. It was wrong, but I didn't care anymore.

One night after a sales call, she and I went to a nightclub in Midland, which was twenty miles from home, and we danced with a few guys. She drank beer, and I drank a coke. I grew up in the 1950s watching *American Bandstand* and would have rather danced than eat. As a young teen, I would go to street dances and dance the evening away to music played from the back of a pickup truck in the neighborhood. These were some of my favorite memories growing up. My husband didn't dance and forbid me to dance at all or even pat my foot on the rare occasion he took me with him to a bar while he hustled pool. As silly as it sounds now, dancing that night was thrilling to me. I knew it was wrong to be there, but I had suddenly stopped liking my husband, and that somehow made it easier, even though I still loved him. I did not drink at all then, and going to a night club was an exciting adventure I really was afraid to repeat. On the way home, my girlfriend and I stopped at a Princess drive-in, and my missing teen years haunted me.

On the drive home between Midland and Odessa, my husband made a U-turn across the highway at one hundred miles an hour and pulled me over. He was coming to find me and was furious, but I didn't think to be scared of him. I was confident in his love and thought he would get over it after awhile. Anyway, I had too much fun that night to be afraid. I was sober, and that was a good thing under the circumstances.

My girlfriend and I left her children and my son with her parents. My husband found them and asked where we had gone. The next morning, I woke to find my husband, our two cars, and the riding lawn mower gone, so I couldn't leave the house. I know taking the riding lawnmower is humorous now, but then I felt completely helpless and abandoned. Our son slept securely in his bed. I got the money together for two plane tickets, left our beautiful home, packed two suitcases, left a lot of my other belongings, and flew back to Houston with our son. I was a little afraid of my father-in-law's power, so I called for a police escort to the Odessa airport.

Another irony was my sister now living back in Houston was separating from her husband at the same time, and we moved into an apartment together in Houston. Without cars, we both got a job near the apartment waitressing in a coffee shop on the feeder of a freeway. We agreed to babysit each other's small children when we worked different shifts. I saved my tips, and in two months, I had enough to buy an old station wagon for $300. That was a lot to save in 1969 from tips and still pay my share of the bills. I would be dressed in a short uniform with my makeup on and hair fixed at 5:00 a.m. when men would come in to drink coffee. I would learn how they liked their coffee and had it waiting on them in front of their regular stool. I made really big tips for a coffee shop. I had learned well how to serve a man during my marriage. I waited on my son's father hand and foot, trying so hard to be the perfect wife.

As soon as I bought the car, I quit the coffee shop, moved in with a widow who was a family friend, and went to work for Battlestein's Department Store in security. I worked undercover to catch employees who were stealing. It seemed like an exciting job while really being very boring, yet had a fairly good salary.

Six months later, one of the two worst days in my life took me completely by surprise!

ONE OF THE WORST DAYS OF MY LIFE

After six months, my son's father called me late one night saying he and his mother were in Houston and desperately wanted to see our son. He told me they wanted to take him to Astro World the next day. I had moved from living with my sister and was living with Ms. Elizabeth, who had been the secretary at the insurance office we lived behind before I started school. She was an elderly widow and a friend of our family. Our five-year-old son was in bed sleeping the night his father surprised me with the phone call. He begged me to bring him to them right then. I did call my Houston attorney, and he advised against it. Against his advice, I woke my baby and gathered some clothes for him, never wanting to keep our son from his father. I took him to his father and grandmother who were waiting in a motel. Today, I often pass that Ramada Inn these forty-four years later and remember that night vividly. I know the very door of the room they were in. What my attorney knew, but didn't tell me, was my husband's attorney had arranged temporary custody before he came to Houston. I will tell you why my attorney kept that from me later.

I woke the next morning to realize I had forgotten to take our baby's shoes because he had been in his footed pajamas. Rushing to dress for work, I planned to stop and deliver his shoes. When I arrived at the Ramada Inn, I found they had checked out. It was alarming, yet I still believed they had taken my baby to the amusement park. I rushed to a club where my eldest brother worked and asked him to help me find them. We looked everywhere: Astro World, all the hotels and motels close by, and every restaurant in a two-mile radius. The level of panic increased throughout the day, and I cannot remember what followed during the next two days. Somehow, I ended up in my car, parked close to my brother's home, and didn't know how I got there. I can only guess I drove all around during that time, in shock, hoping to find my baby. I am still amazed; it was as if I had amnesia. The human mind and emotions has its own protection. On the second day, a policeman stopped to check on me in my parked car, and I couldn't tell him how I got there. After giving him my brother's address, he took me to my married brother's home where I stayed for several days. My brother's love for me was twisted and very possessive. His love was a lot like my husband's love and given the chance would create a prison for me. He wouldn't allow me to leave for days as he controlled my thoughts and actions. He finally released me to go to my mother.

What we did not know during our search was my son's father and grandmother had left that first night to take him away from me. I finally spoke to them by phone after they had returned to their West Texas home days later. They had hidden with him at a friend's home in central Texas in case I came to Odessa looking for them. The days following that conversation were a blurred nightmare. All I can remember is lying on my mother's living room floor, sobbing for days in her one bedroom apartment. I cannot remember anything my mother said to comfort me, but I remember she had an Elvis Presley album of spiritual hymns she played continuously. The Holy Spirit was ministering to me even then.

You may wonder why I didn't follow them to West Texas to get my son back. All I can tell you is I was emotionally broken, afraid, and without any money. It was a dark hole of survival, and I was not rational. Believe me; I've had many moving pictures in my mind of what I could have done. It was God's grace they were only fantasies because in reality, it could have been disastrous. I desperately fought for him legally and will tell you about it later. It was in this desperation that I met a man who promised to help me get my son back. This relationship became another prison for me.

A bitter custody battle and divorce followed, which I will also tell you more about. Needless to say, I carried a lot of anger, hurt, shame, and bitterness in my heart from my childhood and my broken marriage. The deepest bitterness was because my son was taken from me. He was my life! I look back and know our son's father must have felt like I had taken our child away from him in the night when I left our West Texas home. The difference was it had never occurred to me to keep our son from his father, and I believe it was his father's plan to take him from me all along. I don't pretend to know the pain I caused my husband when I left him, but I know now it was almost unbearable for him.

All he returned to me left me desperate to know what to do with the unbearable pain, but remember, I was not walking with my Savior then. Jesus never left me when I left Him, but I was out of touch with the very person I needed most.

My heart broke into a million pieces, and this began the downward spiral of my life for the next nine years. To share those years with you, go with me to a deadlocked room in my heart, and see how Jesus wants us to give Him our worst, before we give Him our best!

BEING FORGIVEN

The brokenness in my heart, the anger, the bitterness, and a self-centered self-destructive mind-set brought me to a daily lifestyle of sin. The heartache and then the guilt and shame of all the sin in my life was a debilitating burden to carry. I do not know who coined the following statement, but it is so true:

> Sin will always take you further than you want to go,
> keep you longer than you want to stay,
> and cost you more than you want to pay!

Beginning to drink alcohol for the first time in my life to drown the pain following the worst day of my life, I entered the nightlife of Houston. I met and entered a relationship with a married man who owned a famous night club in Houston. He promised to help me get my son back no matter what it cost. That's all I needed to hear to begin working for him and have a two-year affair. I desperately wanted someone to love the pain out of me and fill this huge hole in my heart. I mistook his lust and control for love because controlling selfish love is what I had become accustomed to. Being wealthy, he had the money I did not have to fight for my child, and he spent tens of thousands. I vividly remember the day a prominent slick attorney came to his night club to talk with us. When he left, I felt confident he could do anything!

Those years, full of sexual sin, working in a club for eighteen hours a day, and drinking alcohol are a blur. We lived as if we were man and wife. His wife and child lived in one townhouse, and we lived in a townhouse a few miles away. This man and I became pregnant and calculated I would be seven months pregnant when my custody battle went to trial in West Texas. I received advice from friends and chose abortion for our baby. My boyfriend, the baby's father, had promised to divorce his wife and marry me, so I believed having his baby would have worked for our lives if I had not been facing the custody battle. For me, it was not possible to be pregnant then. I didn't really think about the baby in my womb.

We first traveled to Los Angeles and then to Mexico City to get the abortion before settling on an abortionist in Houston. The abortionist punctured my womb causing me to become septic. I passed out under a huge oak tree in his front yard immediately after the procedure. Poison was carried by my bloodstream throughout my body, and two days later, I was rushed to a hospital at the point of death. I was told later my organs were threatening to collapse. I lay in and out of consciousness in that hospital for twenty-one days. My mother found out about the abortion standing outside my open hospital door as several doctors discussed my imminent death and the reasons for it. One of the greatest dangers was there were so many doctors on my case that I was being drastically overdosed with narcotics for pain. By God's amazing grace, I recovered physically but had no idea of the emotional impact abortion had on my life. I knew I was an emotional mess, but amazingly, I did not realize it had anything to do with my abortion.

Within a few months following the abortion, the custody battle and divorce was scheduled. My boyfriend, my mother, and eldest brother flew with my attorney and me to Odessa.

I was allowed to see my son the day before the trial. His father and grandfather brought him to my motel, and I was allowed to play with him in a small park next to the motel for an hour. We played on the swings and just hugged and loved each other as much as we could before it was over. We both cried so hard when it was over. His father and grandfather watched from across the parking lot, and my attorney watched from the other direction. I didn't care for all I could see were my son's loving eyes! When the hour was up, my attorney took him from my arms and returned him to his father. I cried the rest of that day as I remembered my baby's cries for me. I had to get my emotions under control before the trial the next day.

My boyfriend pretended to be on our legal team as he sat at the back of the courtroom. No one ever found out my boyfriend was present or even that he was in my life. My brother pretended to be a private detective. Pretending to be someone he was not was easy for him. I lied about what I did for a living and said I was a bookkeeper. Nothing was ever suggested or proven that I was an unfit mother or that my husband was an unfit father. This was 1970, and my lifestyle might have been grounds to lose my son but it was never discovered.

There was an eleven-man, one-woman jury for the two-day trial. My husband, my attorney, my brother, and boyfriend were the only men in the courtroom who did not wear cowboy boots and a string tie, including the judge. I dressed up the first day in a silver blue silk suit. My attorney instructed me to buy a simple check cotton dress for the second day, but my image was already established, and it didn't fit the West Texas persona. We looked like city slickers, and in West Texas in the 1970s that was a huge mistake. Both attorneys talked as the jury deliberated, and I believed it when they said they both fully believed our son would be given to me. It was hard to take children away from their mother at that time.

On this, the second worst day of my life, the eleven-man, one-woman jury gave full custody to my son's father with no visitation rights for me. This was a shock to everyone! My legal team and I knew something had been arranged behind the scenes. I now know in my heart what happened, yet I have no proof of it.

This is what I believe: My husband belonged to a secret organization that he joined two years before we separated. He would never tell me what it was all about. I have since learned all about it and believe the eleven men on the jury were members of his Masonic brotherhood. I also found out his attorney and the judge were also masons. Now I understand why all eleven men filed out of the courtroom to shake my ex-husband's hand after the verdict. There is a Masonic secret handshake, and at that time, I was completely unaware of the connection.

I remember crying out in the courtroom after the verdict and have been told it was a blood-curdling scream of horrified disbelief. Next, I remember standing on the front steps of the Ector County Courthouse as my ex-husband's entourage drove off honking car horns in victory, and among the cars were some of the jurors. All traces of goodness drained from me at that very moment, and I lived in empty bitterness for years to come.

After returning to Houston without my son, my boyfriend and I paid my attorney to file an appeal. He failed to file it in the allotted time frame. We could not understand this and fired him. I later found out that he was also a mason. He was my second Houston attorney and the third since filing for temporary custody in West Texas before I left. It was shocking to learn all three of my attorneys were masons.

I am not afraid in any way to reveal the masonic influence in my custody case. There was a time when people were afraid of this secret organization, but several books have been published exposing the so-called secrets as well as documentaries on television. It is a secret no more, but they still enslave men by secret oaths. Without Christ, mankind can really be deceived. I know many Christians have made these same oaths and are bound, but if they judged it by God's Word, they would walk away unafraid and renounce it fully. The pastor of the second church Ray and I attended in 1982, had been a worshipful master of the Sugar Land Texas Masonic Lodge and renounced it after his salvation. He made a set of tapes exposing the evil of the organization, which is really a false religion. Exposing the Masonic organization is not the purpose of this book, but it does explain much of what was unexplainable concerning this corrupt trial.

Within a month after the trial and losing my son, I broke up with my boyfriend and began an even more self-destructive life of sin. I went from one man to another and from club to club for work, making a lot of money yet having nothing to show for it. I always dated wealthy men. I figured if I was going to be this miserable, I would do it in style. I can tell you money doesn't help, and in fact, the deception of money can make the pain even worse in many ways.

During these years, I lived in a car, in mansions, and everything in-between. I never stayed in one place for more than four months. I would move out of apartments, taking nothing with me because material possessions meant nothing to me. My life was a series of dark days and crazy nights. I would sleep for days at a time to escape the emotional pain. When I woke, I would start the self-destructive cycle all over again.

When I wasn't working in one club, I would go to another club to party. I would drink myself practically unconscious. Many times I would wonder how I got home or how I wound up where I was that next morning. I can remember many times I would sit at a bar drinking and preaching Jesus to someone who was sitting there in pain like I was. I spent almost every Thanksgiving, Christmas, Easter, Mother's Day, my birthdays, and my son's birthdays getting as drunk as possible. Before I drank so much I couldn't talk, I often told someone about the cross. I can only think now it was because under the influence of alcohol my guard was down and what was planted in my heart as a child came pouring out unrestrained. The amazing thing was, they listened, and we wept together. Then I would drink all the more to drown those emotions too. I was still that abandoned little girl preaching to the shells in the street. But now, it was to shells of empty people. If you are religious, you may think God would never use a drunk. I've learned God will use anything he can to reach the lost, and his callings and gifts are irrevocable (Romans 11:25). We must be careful not to tell God how to bait His hook!

Never in all those years did anyone witness to me about Jesus, and I would not darken the door of a church. I refused to go to weddings or funerals if they were in a church. Many times in the wee hours of the morning I would drive the 610 Loop with a gun and thousands of night club dollars in my purse because I was the manager of the club. I was afraid of no one, yet as I would drive the Loop of Houston, I would turn my head when I was about to pass the exit for my childhood church. Lindale Church is visible from the Loop at the Irvington exit of 610 East, and I feared if I even looked at that church my tough veneer would crumble. I didn't know what that crumble would cause, but I feared it. I was afraid of losing the hardness that I believed protected me. I had broken and wept at that very church altar many times as a child, praying for my alcoholic daddy, and I knew the power of God! Lindale Church is my home church today, and I have since preached from that very pulpit many times. God is a redeemer and restorer! He doesn't repent from calling a heart to ministry, even a child's heart.

I had believed my anger, bitterness, hateful attitude, and tough veneer would protect me. That was such a lie. It was destroying me. I was violently angry! I am sorry to say I put one man in the hospital with my high heel shoe. I didn't know it, but anger unchecked is the driving force to suicide. One night I stood in the middle of the freeway at midnight dressed in a long dark-brown dress and couldn't get hit by a car. I made several attempts at suicide, which failed and had plans for the demise of those I hated. Thank God none of those plans came to fruition. The only explanation I have is God's hand of grace was upon me, and He had plans for my life just like He told the prophet Jeremiah in Jeremiah 29:11.

After losing custody of my child, I quit eating. Depression overwhelmed me. At five feet nine inches, I once weighed eighty-seven pounds. I had never heard about anorexia then, but I was skin and bones. It was at this time I made a decision to run from my pain and everyone I knew. A cocktail waitress friend and I decided to go to Los Angeles, California. I don't remember why we chose LA except she knew someone there. The night we packed for Los Angeles, I first went to my girlfriend's apartment to help her pack. Then we went to my townhouse to pack my belongings. I now look back and once again see God's grace and protection. We entered my townhouse unaware that anyone was there. We went upstairs and began to pack. When I opened the closet door, the man who helped me fight for my son was there pointing a gun at my head with the hammer cocked. Obviously, he would not be abandoned by me, but he didn't realize no one, and not even my life, mattered to me anymore. I had needed this man to fight for my child and to love me, but now I needed no one! My baby whom I loved the most was gone from my life, and I could do nothing about it. So I didn't want anyone's love. I just wanted to run away—away from my broken heart and everyone who reminded me of what I had lost. The problem was I couldn't get away from me! I calmly talked this rejected man out of killing me and probably my friend and himself. I left with him crying and begging for forgiveness for failing to get my child back for me. My heart had so hardened on the steps of the courthouse after the verdict that his plea for forgiveness couldn't reach me. I later revisited it and forgave him and everyone else. Now the struggle was forgiving me!

My time in LA is a blur. I can only remember wandering the streets of Hollywood and drinking in clubs. I took risks that make me tremble today. I don't remember how long I was there, but I moved to Dallas, Texas and began to gain strength and weight. I got all the way up to a size six. Though still way too thin, it was better than below a size two at five feet nine inches. The years that followed were filled with striving to find peace and make sense out of life, which is impossible when you are running from the Savior who gives you peace. I moved back and had many jobs, but mostly in the nightlife of Houston. I married an abusive womanizing man, and it only lasted a few months. After a severe beating

I took from him in our home on Lake Travis, I left with nothing but more of a broken heart and all the money from our bank account.

As I told you, one day a tall, handsome man walked through the doors of the club I worked in. It's funny, before I saw Ray's face I knew he was for me. Two weeks later, he asked me a question, "What would you say if I asked you to marry me?" I didn't play the game of hard to get. I immediately answered, "I would say yes!" So without a ring, I took that as a proposal. It had been a little less than one year since his divorce, and he was scared. This manifested in his refusal to tell his parents about our engagement. We broke up a few months later as I gave him an ultimatum to tell them or we were over. We were over, or so it seemed. On a rare visit from my son in 1978, I was given an opportunity to travel abroad and was given permission to take my eleven-year-old son with me. We left for Paris and then Dubai and Abu Dhabi on the Persian Gulf, followed by Greece and Holland. My son turned twelve on the flight back home after two months abroad. He returned to his father when school started.

I was given a job offer while in Abu Dhabi to be trained as a courier between the Arab sheiks. It was a high-paying job offer, but I now believe it was a trap, and I might never have been heard of again if I had accepted it. I did plan to take the job, and before leaving, I called Ray to say, "I will always love you, and no hard feelings, but I am leaving forever." He quickly made a date with me and proposed. I accepted and married Ray in October 1978. I brought all the pain into our marriage, and it was almost destroyed by 1981. We moved to LaGrange, Texas to run from our troubled marriage. Moving to a small town was a futile attempt to be happy. The thing is your troubles, anger, and heartbreak go with you. I had married a wonderful, kind man, but with me being out of fellowship with Jesus, and Ray unsaved, we didn't have a chance to survive…"But, God!"

We lived in a four-thousand-square-foot house on three acres under ancient oak trees, overlooking rolling hills in LaGrange, Texas. Ray owned a very successful insurance business at that time, and we hoped to sell policies in LaGrange. We drank every weekend, and Ray gambled with friends on the wraparound deck of our beautiful home. When he drank, he was silly and fun but could still win everyone's money playing poker. When I drank, I was mean, jealous, and violent. We were already talking about divorce when one Saturday we argued, and I ran from the house sobbing and walked up the hill to a tiny Catholic church, which had statues outside representing the twelve steps of the cross. Though I had only visited a Catholic church once, I looked at them slowly through tears, and memories of my relationship with Jesus as a child came rushing back. I remember vividly walking back down that hillside street toward our home when suddenly my eyes were open to God's beauty in creation. The sun was setting, the hills were vivid green, and cows were lazily grazing. The huge oak trees were in silhouette against the red-orange sunset sky. It was all stunning to me that day! For the first time in many years, I spoke to God, simply saying, "Wow, Lord, You really did good on this!" Somehow I knew a crack opened in my heart at that very moment. Just to acknowledge that God was my Lord worked a miracle that I wouldn't realize until a few months later.

A few months later, God sent two of his children to witness to us. It was our mechanic and his wife from Houston. They had prayed for us often as our new Cadillac broke down about once a month. We thought we had a lemon for a car, but they knew what God was doing. Each time we took the car to be repaired, they began to pray for us. On this unexpected visit, they asked us how we passed the ninety minutes it took to drive back and forth from our home in LaGrange to our office in Houston. We answered, "I was reading the Book of Mormon to Ray both ways." She shrieked and declared we should stop that immediately because it was a dangerous false religion.

She went to their car and gave us a Christian book titled, *Late Great Planet Earth*[1] by Hal Lindsey. Intrigued it might be sci-fi, we accepted it. She asked for the Book of Mormon in return so she could destroy it. The book they gave us opened the door for Ray's relationship with Jesus and my rededication to my Savior. We are eternally grateful to Rod and Margaret Gorneau for not only the ministry of Hal Lindsey's book but for praying so fervently for us.

Within two weeks of their visit and while reading *Late Great Planet Earth*, Ray accepted Jesus and made him Lord of his life in our car in 1981. Jesus spoke to him on I-10 heading for Houston on a clear October morning. I returned to my Savior after trying to live my life without him since 1963. When Ray accepted Jesus, I came running back to my

Lord so fast it made both our heads swim! When I turned my life back to Jesus, I turned and bumped into my faithful Lord who had never left me all those dark and painful years. We both fell madly in love with the Lord and deeply in love with each other. We did a certain 180-degree turn around and began to love and serve God with all our strength. The drinking and gambling stopped immediately. It is interesting to look back and remember we started reading the Bible in the book of Revelation and devoured it. Then our praying friends gave us a set of tapes by Hilton Sutton, a renowned teacher of the book of Revelation. We listened to all six tapes one Saturday, and we will never forget how it set us on a course to learn all of God's truth.

We tried every small church in LaGrange. Dissatisfied, we moved back to Houston in March 1982. I fell in love with Jesus all over again, and this time with a mature passionate love! I knew in a limited way that God had forgiven me of all the past sin. After all, I certainly begged Him hard enough! But fearing I had not repented for forgotten sins and thus maybe I had not been completely forgiven, I was certainly not free indeed. I think now how foolish my thinking was, as if God didn't already know about every one of my sins and needed me to remind Him. If I had only remembered one sin and confessed just that one sin, God would have seen my repentant heart and cleansed me from all sin (1 John 1:9)! The truth was I had been forgiven from Christ's cross over two thousand years ago! The next heavy burden I carried as a child of God was the struggle to *forgive myself*, and that tormented me for years to come.

AN UNNECESSARY BURDEN

First I want to say something about guilt and shame. I was under the burden of guilt and shame for much of my life. I suffered from shame due to the shameful things done to me and suffered from guilt for the shameful things I did. I can look back and realize shame is spiritually debilitating. Shame makes the head to hang low and the heart to break. Shame kills dreams and leaves the dreamer hopeless. It is the opposite of freedom in Christ and severely limits vision and ministry. Shame leads to sin, not away from it. Shame causes us to try to cover our sin instead of repenting from it.

People without a relationship with God the Father, through God the Son, by the power of God the Holy Spirit may need shame to be a barometer of their sin, but a born-again child of God has the indwelling Holy Spirit to convict them of sin, and he does a much better job than shame and guilt!

I learned from God's grace that when Jesus was made to be all sin (2 Corinthians 5:21, NKJV), He bore my shame on the cross. My guilt was paid for there and I was released from shame. I had walked with the Lord for ten years before I realized I did not have to bear shame any longer. For the redeemed shame is one of the things that passed away when Jesus said, "It is finished!" (John 19:30, NKJV). Because I am in Christ, I am shame free.

Shame is a result of sin and began the moment the first sin was committed. Once Adam and Eve believed the lie of the devil and disobeyed God, they felt shame immediately. Their shame caused them to hide from God and try to cover their sin.

> Then the eyes of both of them were opened, and they knew that they were naked; and they sewed fig leaves together and made themselves coverings. And they heard the sound of the LORD God walking in the garden and they hid themselves from the presence of the LORD God among the trees of the garden. (Genesis 3:7–8, NKJV)

This first couple experienced shame for the first time due to sin, and they hid from God's presence and tried to cover themselves. But God in his mercy killed an innocent animal, shedding innocent blood, and He covered their shame, proving to us we cannot cover our sin and we need a Savior to forgive us, cover us in His holy blood, and set us free. Hiding from God's presence is the greatest tragedy of shame!

> Also for Adam and his wife the LORD God made tunics of skin, and clothed them. (Genesis 3:21, NKJV)

The covenant love of God required that innocent animals be sacrificed to provide garments of skin as a covering for

Adam and Eve. This early foreshadowing of substitutionary atonement points toward the necessity of judgment upon the innocent to provide a covering for the guilty. This temporary covering proceeded throughout the old covenant, but under the new and better covenant, we are clothed with Christ and redeemed by His shed innocent blood.

As Ray and I faithfully sat under the preaching of God's Word, we began to be healed and restored. We served in our church soon after we began to walk with Jesus. At one point, little more than one year after Ray was born again and I rededicated my life to Christ, we served as leaders of three ministries in the small church we attended after moving back to Houston. We led the altar ministry, the hospital visitation ministry with thirty-five volunteers, the intercessory prayer ministry, and we volunteered in the school of ministry. We did not realize our life was not about how hard we could work for God and we should not have been trusted with so much responsibility so soon in our walk with Christ. These leadership positions gave us a false sense of wholeness long before we were truly healed.

Somehow in the midst of all the works of self-righteousness, we failed to learn about the depth of God's grace and His righteousness. We knew grace was God's unmerited, unearned favor but never really thought the concept through in light of God's Word. We were just grateful we were saved by grace without knowing what it fully meant. What we've learned since is life transforming. Go with me to where Paul wrote a profound truth as he was inspired by the Holy Spirit.

> Therefore, if anyone is in Christ, he is a new creation; old things have passed away; behold, all things have become new. (2 Corinthians 5:17, NKJV)

Do you see that Paul wrote "have passed away"? This is past tense because it happened at the cross! My identity now is in Christ! In Christ, in Him, in Christ Jesus is referenced to 165 times in the New Testament. Let's look at what else Paul wrote of this amazing grace. What passed away was our sin nature we inherited from Adam and what became new was God's righteousness becoming our new identity!

> For He made Him who knew no sin to be sin for us, that we might become the righteousness of God in Him. (2 Corinthians 5:21, NKJV)

In 2 Corinthians 5:21, we see that Jesus took our sin nature, which we inherited from Adam, and exchanged it for God's righteous nature, which Adam abdicated to Satan, through sin. *Wow*, this is what I call the great grace exchange!

The great grace exchange is Jesus taking our sin nature we were born with, and inherited from Adam's sin, upon Himself so we can receive God the Father's righteousness and have His nature as Adam and Eve had before they sinned. The blessings is, believers are no longer joint-heirs of Adam's sinful nature but are joint-heirs with Christ and have His nature of righteousness. This is profound truth of who we are as believers in Jesus Christ! And if you are a believer in Jesus Christ and have by faith received Him as your personal Savior, your true identity is also in Christ! We are placed in Christ by the new birth (John 3:3).

Early on, Ray and I learned God forgives us. We seemed to know a lot about forgiveness but actually understood little. So we had much to learn and we still do. We've learned the more you learn about God and His amazing grace, the more you know you need to know!

God's Word has taught us the first way God deals with forgiveness is we must be forgiven by God through trusting what Christ finished on the cross to pay for our sin. It is by God's grace because we could never pay the sin debt we owed. This truth was pretty easily understood; however, it took me years to understand just how forgiven I truly am! I had committed so much sin that I knew I could not bear it. I knew I had to give the guilt of sin to Jesus and accept His forgiveness. I had the cross as an anchor in my life, but I had to learn to give God my worst to make room for His best. So thank God, I finally got it; I was completely and forever forgiven at the cross where my sin was completely paid for! I did not have to beg for God's forgiveness anymore! I owed a debt I could not pay, so God paid a debt He did not owe, leaving no balance owing.

It is interesting that as a four and five-year-old child, my uncle took me with him to minster in the Harris County Jail in 1952. I would sing a song that said that very thing, "I owed a debt I could not pay, He paid a debt He did not owe, I needed someone to wash my sins away. And now I sing a brand new song, Amazing Grace. Christ Jesus paid a debt I could never pay." I learned that song in a revival at Lindale Church when I was only four, but it took half a lifetime to fully accept it.

FORGIVENESS TWO WAYS

Because of the call from God to teach and preach, I've studied God's Word for the past thirty-two years. I've learned He really is a forgiving God. For far too long, my understanding was confused with the legalism religion had mixed with God's grace. One thing about being called to teach and preach, it will keep you searching God's Word and abiding in it until the truth sets you free indeed!

> Then Jesus said to those Jews who believed in Him, "If you abide in My word, you are My disciples indeed. And you shall know the truth, and the truth shall make you free." (John 8:31, 32, NKJV)

Many people quote verse 32 without verse 31. God's truth sets you free as you *abide in it* which means to live in obedience to His truth. God's truth is informative until you live it in your life, at which time, it becomes transformative.

As the years passed and I was abiding in God's Word, I began to learn God had already forgiven me from the cross, and He expected me to forgive everyone who had ever hurt me. I also began to understand these were the only two ways God revealed forgiveness in his Word, yet believing there was a third erroneous way to forgive left me in self-condemnation for years to come. Do not forget, condemnation leads to more sin, not less. Shame leads to more hidden shameful acts, not less. Guilt causes more sinful choices, not less. Let's look at the truth in God's Word.

The two ways God deals with forgiveness:

Number 1: We are forgiven through receiving God's sacrifice of His Son and accepting all our sins were paid for by Jesus' shed holy blood from the cross.

> In Him we have redemption through His blood, the forgiveness of sins, according to the riches of His grace. (Ephesians 1:7, NKJV)

> Much more then, having now been justified by His blood, we shall be saved from wrath through Him. (Romans 5:9, NKJV and so many more Scriptures!)

Number 2: God requires us to forgive everyone the same way we are forgiven by Him.

> Let all bitterness, wrath, anger, clamor, and evil speaking be put away from you, with all malice. And be kind to one another, tenderhearted, forgiving one another, even as God in Christ forgave you. Ephesians 4:31, 32, NKJV.

"And forgive us our sins as we forgive those who sin against us" (Matthew 6:12, NKJV). Jesus was teaching us to pray the Lord's Prayer. If Jesus said to pray, forgive us like we forgive others, we had better get better at forgiving!

Man has added a third way; we are required to forgive, which is neither biblical nor necessary and we will examine it later in this book.

More on the first way God deals with forgiveness. It was easy to discern and understand God so loved me that He gave His only begotten Son to shed His holy blood to forgive me and give me eternal life. I learned John 3:16 as a child and preached it from my front-porch-pretend pulpit before I was in the first grade.

What I did not understand, but God has taught me in recent years, has become the anchor of my teaching ministry. I did not really understand God's grace or His love for years. It was God the Father's great love that sacrificed Jesus on a cross for my sin.

John 3:16 tells us God so loved the world that He gave His only begotten Son! I marked through the word "world" in my Bibles and wrote "me!" God loved Lana so much He gave His only begotten Son! Notice, God so loved! Beloved, God doesn't love us only a little bit, and He demonstrated His great love on a cross. There is no greater love than this!

> But God demonstrates His own love toward us, in that while we were still sinners, Christ died for us! (Romans 5:8, NKJV)

I changed the words here too. From my personal notes, my Bibles now read, "But God demonstrates His own love towards *me*, in that while *I* was still a sinner, Christ died for *me*!"

You see, it is personal to me and I want to remind myself often how much God loves me. I began to learn I am forgiven for one reason: God's great love for me! I hope you will begin to personalize God's amazing grace in your life too. I often teach people to write in their Bibles and will tell them, "After all, you aren't going to return it." I am hard on my Bibles and wear them out quickly, but as they fall apart, the pages are marked in red and highlighted in yellow with handwritten notes throughout and "in Christ" underlined. I refer back to them often and couldn't imagine ever throwing one away even with the pages that have come loose.

I learned from God's Word, and now teach, *all sin was* forgiven at the cross. Not only all my sin before I returned to Jesus, but all sin I will ever commit. For years, I earnestly begged God to forgive me and often wondered if He really could. I do not beg anymore.

What are we saying when we beg God to forgive us? Are we saying we do not completely believe He will? Do we believe He can't or won't? If that is what we believe, then we do not believe His word or completely trust His great love. When I sin, I am truly sorry for it. I own my sin instead of playing the blame game, confess it to God, and thank Him I am forgiven by His grace and completely cleansed by His holy blood. By God's amazing grace, I then turn away from the sin and the opportunity to continue the sin and walk with the Holy Spirit. This is a life of grace and is what John spoke of when he said,

> If we say we have no sin, we deceive ourselves, and the truth is not in us. If we confess our sin, He is

faithful to forgive us our sins and to cleanse us from all unrighteousness. (1 John 1:8, 9, NKJV)

I ask you, does it say anywhere in the above Scripture we must beg God for forgiveness? Does it say we must earn His forgiveness or should worry if He will forgive us again and again? Does it say God forgives some sins and not others? No, when Scripture says we are to confess our sins, it means we are to own it, stop the blame game, confess it to God, and trust God's faithfulness to forgive and cleanse us from all sin!

Notice John said, "all unrighteousness"!

Some Christians fear that fully embracing God's grace will give license to sin. This was a problem with the religious in the Apostle Paul's day, and he dealt with it openly.

What then? Shall we sin because we are not under Law but under grace? Certainly not! (Romans 6:15, NKJV)

I know if you think about this, you will agree people never needed a license to sin. From the Garden of Eden until today, mankind has chosen to sin from a sin nature inherited from Adam and didn't need a license or permission! Born-again believers in Christ are not under the law or slaves to sin but have the righteousness of God! Sin always has been a choice of mankind's free and unsurrendered will. Christians are without excuse when they sin. It is only by choice on this side of the cross of Christ. As believers in Christ and children of God, we may choose sin, but sin no longer has power to choose us.

> For if we have been united together in the likeness of His death, certainly we also shall be in the likeness of His resurrection, knowing this, that our old man was crucified with Him, that the body of sin might be done away with, that we should no longer be slaves of sin. For he who has died has been freed from sin. (Romans 6:5–7, NKJV)
>
> Likewise you also, reckon yourselves to be dead indeed to sin, but alive to God in Christ Jesus our Lord. (Romans 6:11, NKJV)
>
> For sin shall not have dominion over you, for you are not under law but under grace. (Romans 6:14, NKJV)
>
> And being set free from sin, you became slaves of righteousness. (Romans 6:18, NKJV)

Lest we become deceived and believe we have no responsibility in this life of grace, let us read.

> Therefore do not let sin reign in your mortal body, that you should obey it in its lusts. And do not present your members as instruments of unrighteousness to sin, but present yourselves to God as being alive from the dead, and your members as instruments of righteousness to God. (Romans 6:12–13, NKJV)
>
> Do you not know to whom you present yourselves slaves to obey; you are that one's slaves whom you obey, whether of sin leading to death, or of obedience leading to righteousness? (Romans 6:16, NKJV)

Our part is obedience to God, to live our life God's way! Do we know we are set free from our sin nature when we receive Jesus as our Savior and are born again? What really happens when we are born again? We know what happens when we are born naturally the first time. We are born into a family and become children. We receive life, and we begin to live that life and grow in it.

When we are born again, we are placed into God's family by the Holy Spirit and become His children. How? We are born into Christ. We are placed in Christ, and that is our covenant position before God. Just as we grow as physical children, we must also grow as spiritual children.

We must realize that one-third of the Trinity lives within us! God the Holy Spirit went back and forth from heaven to earth to anoint and speak through old covenant believers. After Jesus' work on the cross, and His resurrection and ascension to His throne, God the Father sent God the Holy Spirit to dwell in born-again believers in Jesus. In the old covenant, God had a temple for His people. In the new and better covenant, God has a people for His temple. Wow, what a privilege!

> "Do you not know you are the temple of God and that the Spirit of God dwells in you?" (1 Corinthians 3:16).

The old covenant was between God and mankind. God made a covenant with Abraham, and the Jewish race was born. The new and better covenant is between God the Father and God the Son, and Jesus was born! It is ratified out of their relationship and self-sacrifice by holy blood. This means we are reconciled to God from the position of being in Christ. My identity is not my past guilt and shame, not who or what anyone has said I am, not even what I have said I am, but I am who God says I am in Jesus! It is in this position a born-again believer receives all the benefits and promises of the new and better covenant of grace. Because of what Jesus did on the cross, we are now slaves of righteousness.

It is a historical fact when President Lincoln made the Emancipation Proclamation on September 22, 1862, to free the American slaves; they were at that moment made legally free indeed. The word of it was slow and did not make it from the nation's capitol to the slaves of the Texas Gulf Coast for two years. These freed slaves didn't know the truth, so they lived under the hard taskmasters of slavery. What a tragedy! Yet many Christians live the same way. They allow the hard slave master of sin and the old covenant law to keep them in bondage when all the time a child of God has been set free indeed at the cross. For years, that is how I lived my life in Christ.

> And because you are sons, God has sent forth the Spirit of His Son into your hearts, crying out, "Abba Father".
>
> Therefore, you are no longer a slave but a son, then an heir of God through Christ. (Galatians 4:6–7, NKJV)

God never intended for humanity, created in His image, to be slaves. He created mankind as completely free as He is.

Genesis tells us the Trinity: God the Father, God the Son, and God the Holy Spirit, created mankind in their own image (Genesis 1:26). Mankind was perfect in the Garden of Eden and completely free until Adam and Eve believed the devil's lie that made them doubt God. Mankind went into slavery under Satan at the moment they disobeyed God, yet God had another plan. God the Son was born with human flesh and a sin nature, then lived sinless so He could be made to be sin—so we could be made to be the righteousness of God! Jesus, in human flesh, never sinned for the thirty-three years of His life on earth, not because He couldn't sin, but because He wouldn't sin. Two of the most phenomenal truths in God's Word for me are found in the fifth chapter of 2 Corinthians. Again, I share these with you.

> Therefore if anyone is in Christ, he is a new creation; old things have passed away, behold, all things have become new. (2 Corinthians 5:17, NKJV)
>
> For He made Him who knew no sin to be sin for us, that we might become the righteousness of God in Him. (2 Corinthians 5:21, NKJV)

We need to know what passed away and what became new. We were all naturally born joint-heirs with Adam to a sin nature. Romans 3:23 tells us all have sinned and fallen short of God's glory. We could not be in relationship with a holy God with a sin nature, so God, unwilling to do without us, made a way. In John 14:6, Jesus told us He is the way, the truth, and the life and no one comes to the Father except through Him. That brings us to 2 Corinthians 5:21. Again,

I call it the great grace exchange! Jesus took our sin nature and gave us God's nature, which is His righteousness so we could be reconciled to God the Father who created us. What did Jesus do with the sin nature He took from us? He died to sin once and for all and rose from the dead as the first fruits of the resurrection.

> For when we were still without strength, in due time, Christ died for the ungodly. (Romans 5:6, NKJV)

> But now Christ is risen from the dead, and has become the first fruits of those who have fallen asleep. (1 Corinthians 15:20, NKJV)

First, we need to know when the Bible speaks of believers falling asleep it means we have eternal life and death is only physical. To better understand first fruits, we must know that in Leviticus the old covenant believers would harvest the first sheaf of grain, take it to the priest, and he would wave it before the Lord consecrating the harvest to Him. First fruits were also proof of a harvest to come. Jesus was the first to be resurrected from death to give us eternal life and is proof of a harvest of souls to come. Without the resurrection of Jesus Christ, we are without hope for eternal life with God! Paul wrote of what that tragedy would be like.

> And if Christ is not risen, your faith is futile; and you are still in your sins! Then also those who have fallen asleep in Christ have perished. If in this life only we hope in Christ, we are of all men the most pitiable. But now Christ has risen from the dead, and has become the first fruits of those who have fallen asleep. (1 Corinthians 15:17–20, NKJV)

This leaves no need for self-righteousness. It is by grace that we have God's nature as Adam and Eve did before the fall. So since all have sinned and fallen short of the glory of God, we needed a Savior. And a Savior has been provided by the grace of God through His great love.

Paul tells us in Colossians 1:27 (NKJV), "To them God willed to make known what are the riches of this mystery among the Gentiles: which is Christ in you, the hope of glory."

Being a new creation means we have God's nature instead of a sin nature. Can we still sin? Yes, just as Adam and Eve had free will when they sinned in a perfect environment and in a perfect relationship with God. They chose to sin, and we can choose sin also, but we do not have to. We are not dominated by a sin nature if we are in Christ. We have to choose to reject temptation to sin by an act of our free will surrendered to God, resisting the devil, and he has no choice but to flee! (James 4:7). Be careful that you live this entire Scripture, "Therefore submit to God. Resist the devil and he will flee from you." If we try to resist the devil without submitting in obedience to God, we will have no authority over the devil.

> Likewise you also, reckon yourselves to be dead to sin, but alive to God in Christ Jesus our Lord. (Romans 6:11, NKJV)

> For sin shall not have dominion over you, for you are not under law but under grace. (Romans 6:14, NKJV)

It is freedom not only from knowing God's Word but by abiding in the knowledge of His Word. To abide means to believe God's Word and live like it is the truth. Just "knowing" doesn't set us free. Knowing truth is information. Living God's truth is transformation. The Gulf coast slaves had to believe they were freed and then act on what they finally learned. They had to change their lives and live a new life of freedom. Not all of them believed it when they received the good news, and history tells us many legally freed slaves died in slavery due to unbelief.

The Bible calls grace being joint-heirs with Christ in Romans 8:16–17, NKJV, "The Spirit Himself bears witness with our spirit that we are children of God, and if children, then heirs—heirs of God and joint—heirs with Christ."

What are we heirs to? We are heirs to every promise and every privilege of the new and better covenant of grace, which the Father established with His Son on the cross and ratified by His holy blood! We are also joint-heirs with Christ by being in Christ. In this new and better covenant between the Father and the Son, we share in the benefits.

> "But now He has obtained a more excellent ministry, inasmuch as He is also Mediator of a better covenant, which was established on better promises" (Hebrews 8:6, NKJV).

Wow, that is better news than anything you will ever hear! You are not only forgiven, you are established in right relationship with God in Christ.

> Hebrews 12:2 (NKJV) tells us, "Looking unto Jesus the author and finisher of our faith, who for the joy that was set before Him endured the cross, despising the shame, and has sat down at the right hand of the throne of God."

What possible joy could have been set before Jesus as He endured the horrendous humiliation and indescribable agony of the whip and the cross? You and I were the joy! Because of God's sacrifice of His Son, we have the right to become God's children too, and that was the joy Jesus focused on as He endured it all. For Him to focus on new covenant believers being righteous as Adam and Eve were created before the fall, was joy to Jesus and a joy strong enough for Him to endure all the cross brought to Him: body, soul, and spirit. Think on that. You are that important to God!

It would take a volume of books to write enough about the cross, and it would still be too deep a truth to exhaust. It was an indescribable day of suffering for our Savior! I believe it is imperative to know, what we are humanly capable of knowing about what Jesus suffered in order for us to understand God's grace.

I will share more of my life with you, but first I want to share a little of what really happened the day all of history was eternally changed; the day Jesus was crucified for you and for me. I take you to the bloody cross where Jesus paid for you, not to traumatize you, but so you will know your value in Christ. The value of anything is set by the price paid for it. You could hold something of immeasurable value in your hand and think it is "take it or leave it" until you know what the price is.

I rarely recommend a book other than the Holy Bible, but I highly recommend *The Darkness and the Dawn* by Charles R. Swindoll,[2] published by Insight for Living, www.insight.org. It is the most powerful book I have personally read on the cross. We do not find graphic descriptions of crucifixion in the four Gospels: Matthew, Mark, Luke, and John. It was too horrendous for these men who loved Jesus to pen in their gospels. To know what happened takes a study of Roman crucifixion. Dr. Swindoll's book gives true historic accounts of what scourging with a flagellum and crucifixion does to a human body.

The night Jesus was arrested; He shared His last Passover meal with His disciples. The next day was the Day of Atonement where the Jewish race could know their sins were covered for one more year. Judas left to betray Jesus after Jesus washed the feet of all twelve disciples, including Judas. Think of that; Judas running through the dark streets of Jerusalem with damp feet, which still had the sensation of Jesus' loving hands washing them and the warmth of Jesus' tears. I believe Jesus, knowing Judas would betray Him, washed Judas' feet with the water from the basin mixed with His warm tears.

After Judas left, Jesus instituted the Last Supper we call Communion. For the first time, the bread Jesus broke at Passover represented His body, which just a few hours later would be broken by scourging and crucifixion. When Jesus lifted the bread and broke it, He was representing the old covenant that was passing away. God had prepared Him a body of flesh to complete and fulfill the old covenant between God and man. The Jewish matzo bread we break today is the same as the Matzo bread Jesus broke that night. It is unleavened flat bread with grill marks on it that resemble the bloody stripes that would be on Jesus' back after He was beaten the night He was arrested. I cannot look at it without remembering.

When Jesus lifted the cup of wine that night it no longer represented the blood of the slaughtered lambs the Jewish people put on the outside doorframes of their dwelling in Egypt. Jesus told them the bread was His broken body for them and as He lifted the cup of wine He told them it represented His holy blood, shed for them. It represented a new and better covenant!

When they finished the ceremonial meal, Jesus walked with them to a garden where He was accustomed to go to pray. It was a garden on the Mount of Olives, called Gethsemane, which meant *oil press*. It was so fragrant with flowers that organic fertilizer was prohibited and the garden was kept locked. Joseph of Arimathea, a rich ruler in the government of Israel and a secret follower of Jesus, must have owned it, for his personal tomb was in this garden. This is the borrowed tomb Jesus was buried in. On our trip to Israel in 1994, my husband and I stood in this borrowed, empty garden tomb, carved into the hillside. Once you enter, there is no doubt it was the tomb from which Jesus was resurrected. We knew by Scripture and by the Holy Spirit we were in the empty tomb where the dead body of our

Savior had been laid and wrapped in burial cloths and was raised from death. It was a life-altering experience, and we wept tears of joy.

Jesus fought the spiritual battle of the ages in this garden the night He was arrested. As His disciples slept a few feet away, Jesus battled so fervently in prayer that the capillaries in His head burst and His blood mixed with His sweat and tears (Luke 22:44). He was resisting a temptation stronger than any we will ever experience. He resisted the temptation to exercise His free human will to escape the purpose His Father had given Him to fulfill. This is when and where the battle for our soul was won! This is where the devil lost the battle as Jesus submitted to an unimaginable cup of separation from the Trinity as He received the full wrath of God for sin only hours away. Sin would soon separate Him from His Father and the Holy Spirit for three horrendous hours of dark agony on the cross. Many of us have thought the cup Jesus was asking His Father to take away was the cross, but no, it was the separation by sin from the Trinity for three immeasurable hours. His surrendered will to His Father's will was what won this indescribable spiritual battle. And it is our surrender to God's will that will win our victories. There is no other way!

> Then He came to them a third time and said to them, "Are you still sleeping and resting? It is enough! The hour has come; behold, the Son of Man is being betrayed into the hands of sinners" (Mark 14:41, NKJV).

...But, I Can't Forgive Myself

What was enough? Jesus' submission to His Father's will was enough to see Him through the agony of the cross and the separation from the Trinity by sin.

As soldiers led by Judas approached the garden, Jesus assured His disciples He had prayed through and said, "It is enough!" If you have heard the terminology "pray through" and wondered what it meant, it means to pray until you have sincerely and completely surrendered your will to God's will. What was Jesus referring to when He said, "It is enough"? He meant His surrendered will was enough to get Him to and through the cross where He finished what He had come to earth to do, to give us salvation and eternal life as well as a new and better covenant in Him. *Wow*, the power of submissive prayer!

Jesus was arrested at midnight and endured a long night of interrogation in seven illegal trials. During these hours, one of His closest friends denied he even knew Jesus. Peter had slept instead of watching and praying in Gethsemane and now failed Jesus. He denied he even knew Jesus, due to fear. This hurt Jesus, but it broke Peter's heart. It gives us great hope to see it was God's grace that later restored Peter to his former position on the shore of the Sea of Galilee as his risen Savior gave him three chances to say he loved Him. Then Jesus commissioned the restored Peter to ministry. Peter's restoration was so complete that he later died a painful death instead of denying Christ ever again (John 21:1–19, NKJV).

In the predawn hours before Jesus was crucified, He was mocked by men as a cohort of Roman soldiers pulled His beard from his face while spitting on him. A Roman cohort consisted of 480 legionnaires with 6 centurions. We are not told if they all spat in Jesus' bleeding face, but if only a few did, it was humiliating. Their spittle mixed with His holy blood as it ran down His face mingling with His tears. He spoke not one word. The soldiers made a crown from kindling dried from a bush with six-to-eight-inch razor-sharp thorns and pressed it into His scalp and brow to mock Him as King of the Jews. They stripped Jesus completely naked and put a *chlamus* (short cape) around His shoulders and called it His kingly robe. They beat Him about His head with a stick they gave Him for a scepter. Isaiah prophesied about Jesus' being beaten, spat on, and about His beard being plucked from His cheeks:

> "I gave my back to those who struck Me, and My cheeks to those who plucked out the beard; I did not hide My face from shame and spitting" (Isaiah 50:6, NKJV).

A careful historical and medical study of the cruel practice of scourging reveals what really happened to Jesus the morning of His crucifixion.

From the JAMA (Journal of American Medical Association) and other documented resources: for scourging, the Roman soldiers shackled Jesus' hands and feet to the ground as He was bent over what was called the stump. The stump was about the height of a fire hydrant and nothing like the post we've seen Jesus tied to in movies. Two soldiers (called Lictors), who had been well trained in the torture of the flagellum (whip), positioned themselves behind Jesus and lifted the whip, and began to whip Jesus mercilessly. As the two strong Roman soldiers repeatedly struck Jesus' back, the metal balls would cause deep contusions, and the leather thongs of the whip and the sharp sheep bone would cut into the subcutaneous tissues. Then as the flogging continued, the lacerations would tear into the underlying skeletal muscles and would produce quivering ribbons of bleeding flesh. This practice of torture was designed to reduce a victim's strength to hasten death upon crucifixion.

Most men lost consciousness at the stump, and many died. When a man would lose consciousness from the excruciating pain from this cruel beating, a bucket of strong salt water would be splashed on his wounds to revive him to consciousness to suffer further torture. The Jews had a law prohibiting more than forty lashes.[345]

The Romans had no law limiting the number. The lead balls tied to the leather straps of the whip would cause deep contusions and bruises to weaken the flesh so the sharp edges of sheep bone and metal would pull the flesh from the body, even exposing the victim's bones and organs. The leather strips would lash around the torso so the body and extremities were torn to ribbons, front and back. Yes, this is what the prophet Isaiah foretold 740 years before Christ's birth.

> But He was wounded for our transgressions, He was bruised for our iniquities; the chastisement for our peace was upon Him, and by His stripes we are healed. (Isaiah 53:5, NKJV)

The Roman government intended crucifixion and what led up to being crucified to be as publically humiliating as possible to deter crime against Rome. Jesus was completely naked when He was whipped. After the beating, Roman soldiers put Jesus' outer garment back on His bloody body and led Him through the streets of Jerusalem. The same route is now called the Via Dolorosa, meaning, the way of suffering. Jesus carried His cross in the center of four soldiers led by a centurion to a high hill. His dehydration and blood loss made Him fall under the weight of the crossbeam. A Gentile man named Simon of Cyrene carried the crossbeam the rest of the way to a hill, which is called Golgotha in Hebrew and Calvary in Latin. It is known as the place of the skull or skull hill because there are recesses in the front of the rocky hill that resemble a human skull. There, they stripped Jesus naked again and gambled for His seamless outer garment. Victims of crucifixion were hung naked. It's poignant to think of Jesus bearing the shame of nakedness in public, which caused Adam and Eve to hide from Him in the garden of Eden. The crucifixion detail nailed His wrists and feet to a cross, between two criminals. There is much more to know about crucifixion, and it is a life-changing study but is too much for this small book. Come with me now to Calvary, and listen to the biblical account of what Jesus said from His cross.

When someone significant in our lives is dying, the one thing we want to hear most is their last words. So let's lean close and listen to the seven statements Jesus made from His cross, which were the last words He spoke before dying. Lean in and listen!

First, Jesus spoke to His heavenly Father and made an amazing statement of grace.

> "Father, forgive them because they do not know what they are doing." (Luke 23:34, NKJV)

Secondly, Jesus spoke to the repentant thief crucified next to Him.

> "I assure you today you will be with Me in paradise." (Luke 23:43, NKJV)

Thirdly, concerned for His mother after His death, Jesus spoke to her and His disciple John, saying, "Woman, he is your son… she is your mother" (John 19:26–27, NKJV).

This third statement ended what Jesus said prior to being made to be sin!

Here we must consider; before Jesus made His fourth statement, the entire earth grew dark. All sin was placed on Jesus, as well as, all disease. Do not go on from this scene without trying to realize what all sin was! With our finite minds, we cannot fully imagine what it looked like for a man to be made to be *all* sin and *all* disease at once. As Jesus bore all sin and all disease on the cross, the earth grew utterly dark. His Father's eyes were too holy to look upon Jesus as he was made to be sin.

Isaiah, trying to describe this scene 740 years before, prophesied what Jesus would look like for the three hours from noon until 3:00 p.m.

> So His visage would be marred more than any man,
> And His form more than the sons of men. (Isaiah 52:14, NKJV)

It is important for us try to imagine for a moment what Jesus must have looked like after the horrendous beating, after His beard was torn out, eight-inch thorns pressed into His scalp, and His flesh hung in bloody ribbons. Then see His wrists and feet nailed to a rough, used cross and bleeding. In this condition, try to imagine *all* sin and *all* diseases placed upon Him. No, we cannot imagine this, but it is imperative to try so we will understand and never doubt God's unimaginable love as He crucified His only Son for us. If we face this, we can always humbly take our doubt, our fears, our guilt and shame, and all our sin to the cross where we were forever forgiven!

The Message Bible says, "He didn't even look human—a ruined face, disfigured past recognition" (Isaiah 52:14).

> "For He made Him who knew no sin to be sin for us, that we might become the righteousness of God in Him" (2 Corinthians 5:21).

It was such a horrendous and hideous sight, the sun Jesus created could not shine on Him, and Jesus hung there in utter darkness for three unbearable hours. His Father became a judging God to Him as God judged all sin in Him.

> Now it was about the sixth hour, and there was darkness over all the earth until the ninth hour. Then the sun was darkened and the veil in the Temple was torn in two. (Luke 23:44–45, NKJV)

(Third hour was 9:00 a.m., sixth hour was noon, and ninth hour was 3:00 p.m.)

Every evil act of mankind was placed on Jesus. All sin! Jesus' Father poured out His entire wrath against sin on His Son! Jesus absorbed God's entire justifiable wrath against sin. If you believe God is mad at you, you have not visited these three hours where God's entire wrath was poured out on His Son so He would not have to pour it out on you!

Because of the finished work of the cross, believers are not appointed to God's wrath; however, those who reject God's sacrifice of His Son are. Right after John 3:16, Jesus speaks about the wrath of God against those who reject Him.

> He who believes in Him is not condemned; but he who does not believe is condemned already, because he has not believed in the name of the only begotten Son of God. (John 3:18, NKJV)

Remember, scripture tells us that Jesus never sinned but for those three hours, He was *made* to be sin! Jesus was nailed to the cross at 9:00 a.m., but at high noon, the earth grew utterly dark for the next three hours until Jesus finished what He came to earth to do, and He gave up His spirit at 3:00 p.m. No one killed Jesus. The Jews who said, "Crucify Him!" and the Roman soldiers who beat and nailed Him to the cross did not kill Jesus. The soldier that pierced Jesus' side with a sword did not kill Jesus, for He was already physically dead. The water and blood that gushed from His dead heart muscle is absolute medical proof His physical body was dead. No human being had the power to kill the

Author of Life against His will. Crucifixion did not kill Jesus. Jesus gave up His life willingly for us.

At the moment Jesus was made to be sin and for the first and last time in all eternity, He did not address His father as "Father" but addressed His Father as "God" during these hours of being forsaken! Jesus was forsaken by God as He was judged for our sin. Jesus, becoming all sin, was forsaken by God so we won't be. Think on that!

For a moment in eternity, Jesus could hardly bear the separation from God His Father and God the Holy Spirit, and He called out in a loud voice in His native language of Aramaic, making His fourth dying statement,

> "Eloi, Eloi, lama sabachthani?" That is, "My God, My God, why have You forsaken Me?" (Matthew 27:46, Mark 15:34, NKJV; Jesus was actually quoting God's Word in Psalm 22:1)

It is profoundly significant that for the first and last time in eternity Jesus addressed His Father as God! While Jesus was forsaken by His Father because He had been made to be all sin, He was being judged for all sin by a holy God.

Fifthly, Jesus revealed His humanity and simply said,

> "I am thirsty." (John 19:28, NKJV)

Next, in His sixth statement, Jesus declared by three profound words the ratification of the new and better covenant between Himself and His Father,

> "It is finished!" (John 19:30, NKJV)

Then, knowing all He came to do was accomplished, His seventh and final statement was not addressed to a judging God, but again to His Father as Jesus gave up His life and said,

> "Father, I entrust My spirit into Your hands!" (Luke 23:46, NKJV)

It is highly significant here to see when Jesus' work on the cross was finished He again called God "Father." This is further evidence that Jesus finished all that was necessary for your sin and my sin to be forgiven, and all that was required for us to be reconciled to God, and for us to be made His beloved children and given the right to call God Father. Beloved child of God, all our sin was forgiven there, at that moment!

A born-again child of God is not forgiven when they beg God to forgive them. We were forgiven when Jesus said, "It is finished!" We receive this forgiveness when we repent for sinning, which is to be truly sorry and go the other way from the sin.

Like no other words ever spoken, each of these words, being the last seven statements spoken by the One who spoke the universe into being, requires recognition and remembrance. Then to think of the agony He was in when He chose these words makes them even more poignant, precious, and powerful.

The thought that Jesus had you and me on His mind as He endured the cross, to ensure a relationship between His Father and us, is beyond our ability to fully comprehend with our finite mind. We can only, by faith, wrap our heart around the truth of it. I am convinced there are no more powerful words that could come into our life than Jesus' words, "It is finished!"

You and I being redeemed and reconciled to God the Father were the joy set before Jesus (Hebrews 12:2). Our becoming God's forgiven child was the prize Jesus focused on as He was beaten, tortured, crucified, and forsaken by God. God the Father accepted His Son's sacrifice, which is proven by Jesus' resurrection and position at God's right hand. Jesus said, "It is finished!" and God accepted it fully. It is settled for eternity! Let us never forget a vital part of Jesus' sacrifice was to submit to being made to be all sin, and part of our Father's sacrifice was to be willing to pour all of His wrath on His Son.

When Jesus prayed in the Garden of Gethsemane the night before His crucifixion and momentarily asked His Father if the sin and separation cup could pass from Him, He was talking about separation from the Trinity. He knew He faced this unimaginable three hours where He would be all alone and forsaken by His Father and His Holy Spirit, yet He submitted to His Father's will for you and for me. What great love the Father, the Son, and the Holy Spirit has for us!

It was on this cross, on this hill in Israel, in utter darkness that we were forgiven and healed. It is finished! So looking at the cross and listening to Jesus' last words should settle forever that you are forgiven if you are a born again child of God.

This is one of the two ways God deals with forgiveness, by grace, and we should praise Him that we are forever forgiven. This profound, unchangeable truth should compel every believer in Christ to run to God and quickly repent of sin! Repentance does not mean to beg God for forgiveness. Repentance means to turn and abandon sin and go the other way from it.

> "If we confess our sins, He is faithful and just to forgive us our sins and to cleanse us from all unrighteousness" (1 John 1:9).

GOD REQUIRES US TO FORGIVE!

I was set up by the devil for destruction from my earliest memory. I now know God had a call on my life to teach and preach His Word to wounded people from before I was in my mother's womb.

I remind you, God told Jeremiah, "Before I formed you in the womb I knew you; before you were born I sanctified you; I ordained you a prophet to the nations" (Jeremiah 1:5, NKJV).

Yes, I was ordained by God too, not as a prophet to the old covenant nations, but as a minister of His cross, His grace and healing wherever He gives me an opportunity. He also knew me from before I was in my mother's womb. Before you say, "Oh, Lana, get over yourself," you need to know God knew you and planned your life to be blessed before you were born. He reminded Jeremiah later that He had wonderful plans for him in Jeremiah 29:11. You may not be surrendered to God's plan for your life at this time, but that does not mean He doesn't have one, and His plan is far better than ours!

Each of us needs Gethsemane's surrender to God's will daily to have His purpose realized in our lives. Usually my Gethsemane is a large yellow flowered chair, which by the way matches nothing in my home. Interestingly, my Garden of Gethsemane chair is flowered. I call it my Jesus chair, and it is perfect for me. Next to it I have a few of my Bibles, my journal, a red pen where I listen to Him on purpose and write what He tells me, a box of tissues, and sometimes a carefully chosen Christian book or devotional. I have a CD player close by with worship music. It is usually in this chair I struggle and pray through to surrender my will to my heavenly Father's will. The battles in my life are fought there and victories won. You may not have a specific private place in your home for a Jesus chair, but there needs to be a place. Jesus went to a *place* He was accustomed to pray to fight the battle for our eternal souls. I so highly recommend you pray and ask God for your Gethsemane place and then value it highly and visit it daily. The heart of God's plan for every life is that we accept all Jesus did on the cross to make us His children.

I shared with you, in my pretend childhood world, where I escaped from abuse in my imagination; I often pretended I was a preacher. I remember though the messages I pretended to preach were simple, they were really good. That's because it was all about Jesus. At five and six years old, that's all I knew. Now here I am in my sixties teaching and preaching the Gospel of Jesus Christ with passion, and it is still all about Jesus, and I know it is all I need to know.

God's enemy got a glimpse of my calling from God before I was in the first grade of school. The devil began to bring people into my life to destroy my innocence and set me up for the tragedy of sin before I could walk in God's calling and plan for me. Well, the devil's plans always backfire on him. Let's remember he is a loser with capital *L*! He is a zero with the rim knocked off! This is key: his plans for you will fail as you surrender your will to God. If Jesus needed Gethsemane's surrender, we should know we must have the same, and often!

God made a way on the cross for me to be forgiven, healed, and restored to His calling. All the devastation that was in Satan's plan for me is now treasure God uses for His purpose in my life and ministry to other broken lives. This is what Jesus meant as He opened the scroll of Isaiah and read Isaiah 61. Then in Luke 4:18, it is recorded Jesus read where Isaiah prophesied the Spirit of the *Lord* was upon Jesus to give us beauty for ashes, the oil of joy for mourning, and a garment of praise for the spirit of heaviness. He takes the ashes of our sinful lives and transforms them to the beauty of His purpose in our lives. I am so grateful God took the trash of my life and turned it to treasure for others!

So now we understand by God's Word; God's grace made us free. Still there is a way God gives us to stay free.

Being forgiven by God makes us free but forgiving others keeps us free!

Knowing what unforgiveness and bitterness does to us, God requires us to forgive everyone for everything the way He forgives us for everything. Paul writes to the Colossians:

> Therefore, as the elect of God, holy and beloved, put on tender mercies, kindness, humility, meekness, longsuffering; bearing with one another, and forgiving one another, if anyone has a complaint against another; even as Christ forgave you, so you also must do. (Colossians 3:12–13, NKJV)

Did you notice the last five words are "so you also must do"? The root word for forgiving is *charis*, which is Greek for "grace." My simple definition of grace is receiving from God what we do not deserve. And God asks us to give to others the forgiveness they may not deserve.

The word *forgiving*, in Colossians 3:13, is an act in which one person releases another from an offense: (1) refusing to enact the penalty due him or her, (2) refusing to consider the cause of the offense, and (3) refusing to allow the offense to effect the relationship (The New Spirit Filled Life Study Bible, NKJV, page 1675).

Because of the cross, God refused to enact the penalty due to us for sin. Because of the cross, God did not consider the cause of our offense against Him and forgave us for sin whether we meant to sin or not. Because of the cross, we are reconciled to a loving relationship with Him.

We also need to see where Jesus gave His disciples a pattern for prayer and in Matthew 6:12; Jesus said to ask our Father in heaven to forgive us just like we forgive others. Whoa, then we better get better at forgiving! Have you prayed this well known prayer so much and so fast that you failed to see how Jesus said to ask for forgiveness?

> In this manner therefore pray: Our Father in heaven, Hallowed be Your name. Your kingdom come.
> Your will be done on earth as it is in heaven. Give us this day our daily bread.
> *And forgive us our debts,*
> *As we forgive our debtors.*
> And do not lead us into temptation, but deliver us from the evil one. For Yours is the kingdom and the power and the glory forever. Amen. (Matthew 6:9–13, NKJV)

Notice, without taking a break in giving us the Lord's pattern for prayer in Matthew 6:9–13, Jesus went on to speak to us more about forgiving others.

> For if you forgive men their trespasses, your heavenly Father will also forgive you. But if you do not forgive men their trespasses, neither will your heavenly Father forgive your trespasses. (Matthew 6:14–15, NKJV)

The Amplified Bible says from the original language of these verses, "If you forgive people their trespasses [willful and reckless sins, leaving them, letting them go and giving up resentment] your heavenly Father will forgive you" (Matthew 6:14–15).

This means to forgive people who sin against us whether they meant to or not. While thinking this isn't a fair requirement, let's remember we are forgiven by God whether we meant to sin against Him or not.

Verse 15 is clear; if we do not forgive others, we are not forgiven. In the beginning, I asked you to read this little book with your Bible open. Please turn to Matthew 18:21–35 and read the parable Jesus gave us to emphasize the importance of forgiving others. Then join me again in this book.

Now that you have read this story, let me list a few points Jesus made:

- The master had a right to settle accounts.
- Neither man could pay his debt, neither the great debt nor the small debt.
- When the man who owed the master a great debt repented and asked for mercy, the debt was completely forgiven by the king.
- When the freed forgiven man went out and found someone who owed him a small debt, he had no mercy and demanded payment.
- The forgiven man refused to forgive!
- Others saw this, and it hurt the forgiven man's testimony.
- Others told the master, and it made him very angry.
- The freed forgiven man again went into the bondage of unforgiveness where there is torment.

Here, Jesus wants us to see ourselves, forgiven by God yet unwilling to forgive. We are made free by God's grace but cannot stay free unless we forgive. This is a key to walking in the freedom of grace. God sets us free from His righteous judgment, but we stay free by releasing others from our judgment.

I must make this perfectly clear: believers are not forgiven and admitted to heaven because they forgive others, nor are they unforgiven and excluded from heaven for not forgiving others. That is not what Jesus meant in Matthew 6:14 and 15. We were forgiven at the cross, not dependent on what we do, but completely dependent on what Jesus did in His finished work on the cross for us. What unforgiveness interrupts is our communion and fellowship with God. When we ask God to forgive us while holding onto unforgiveness for another, we ask God to forgive us while we deliberately withhold forgiveness, which is sin.

I spent so many years refusing to forgive my abusers, my son's father and his parents, the attorneys, the jury, the judge, and others. I was tormented by my own unforgiveness. You may have heard it said that unforgiveness is like taking poison every day expecting it to kill someone else. The point is it may hurt others, but it will always hurt you far more. Some may say it feels good to hate someone who hurt them, but a closer look at their life will reveal the pain hate produces in them. Our freedom is God's motive in requiring us to forgive. Yes, it is His will that our forgiveness leads our offenders to freedom in Him, but that may or may not occur as it depends on them. There is one thing we can be sure of, forgiving will keep us free.

There is a real power in forgiving! It is empowering to live a life of forgiveness. I even had to forgive dead men, and men whose names I could no longer remember. Some of my abusers died before I began to walk in obedience to God to forgive them. If they were dead, you may ask, "Why forgive them?" They obviously did not benefit from my forgiveness but I sure did! You see, they cannot continue to abuse me in my bitter memories anymore and that is being free indeed. It is so liberating to live life without anger, hatred, and bitterness.

I am so thankful for the revelation that forgiving others is empowering to me and will in some cases lead others to forgiveness from God. Free is a wonderful way to live! Nothing, absolutely nothing, is worth the torment of unforgiveness to me.

I want to be clear: God is not asking you to be vulnerable to more hurt and the possibility of abuse from the ones you forgive. It is a matter of the purity of your heart, and that is why Jesus says to forgive from our heart.

By God's grace, I was able to forgive my son's father for all the pain. I came to understand I had hurt him too when I left our home in West Texas to come back to Houston with our child. It was a remarkable day when my son's father and his wife and Ray and I shared our son's two children at Sea World in San Antonio, Texas for two days. Forgiving them had set me free to see them again and share our grandchildren. I do not know if my former husband has forgiven me from his heart. We are civil to each other, but only God knows his heart. I hope so for his sake. I pray he will know freedom in Christ as I do.

Over the years, as our son was being raised by his father, I was summoned to come to their home to help with our son's emotional turmoil. I would go, stay in their home, and do the best I could to help him only to have to leave again and fly back to my turbulent life in Houston. I would go, but I would go with a heart of well-hidden unforgiveness, hatred, and bitterness.

So the day I forgave my son's father, his wife, and his parents from my heart, all the rejection, heartbreak, and pain in my life was given to God at the foot of His Son's bloody cross. That was a major turning point for me. I rejoice that God made a way for me to stay free indeed by forgiving!

"BUT I CAN'T FORGIVE MYSELF"

Now to get to the point of the title of this book! We have looked at being forgiven by God and forgiving others, but what about forgiving ourselves? You and I hear it all the time. We hear we must forgive ourselves or should forgive ourselves. We even hear that God expects us to forgive ourselves. That sounds so right and righteous.

I ask you here, do you know of even one verse of Scripture telling you to forgive yourself or how to do it?

I believed I needed to forgive myself for years, and it became the greatest struggle of my life. I even recommended it to many people, counseling, "Jesus forgave you, and you must forgive yourself." It sounded so right while being so wrong. I hope and pray, by a miracle of God, everyone I mistakenly told to forgive self will read this book or hear the truth from someone else.

All the years I struggled to forgive myself and told others to do the same; I knew it wasn't something I knew how to do. Now I know why. There is no Scriptural instruction for this much-recommended exercise of self-forgiveness, which is really self-righteousness and humanism that has crept into church doctrine.

I am not about to say here that abortion is worse than any other sin. You may think it is, but God doesn't. He had to shed His precious holy blood for the gossip too; however, I will say for me, emotionally, it was far harder to release the shame and guilt of abortion than any other sin in my life. For a woman or man who has chosen to end the life of their baby or babies, it is very hard to even try to desire to forgive self, and when we see it is impossible, there is a great danger.

The real danger in the impossibility of forgiving yourself is beginning to doubt God can or will really forgive you!

To hide my sexual sin, I had my first abortion. Prior to the abortion procedure, I thought of my baby as *the impossible situation*. The moment it was over, I thought of my baby as *my baby*. The guilt was overwhelming!

When I lost custody of our precious son to his father in court, my world came apart like a huge tornado hit it. At a very early age, sexual abuse had taught me sex equaled love in some perverted way. So I grew up to think if I could not drown my pain in alcohol I wanted someone to love it out of me. The sinful relationships I had were from lust and were never true love. I was still looking for the love I lost at five when my daddy left us and the love I continued to lose every time a hero in my little life abused me.

Three years after my first abortion, I became pregnant again. This time, I didn't know who the father was. I was living a self-destructive, promiscuous lifestyle and rarely saw the light of day. Guilt, anger, and bitterness were in the driver's seat of my life. Though abortion nearly killed me the first time, when I went for a second abortion three years later I didn't care if it killed me. I believed I had nothing to live for and was suicidal. I look back on those years and marvel that so many people thought I was on top of the world. I traveled, had big cars, had fancy clothes and jewelry, but what I gave up for that lifestyle was very costly. I didn't even want to live.

I went to an obstetrician in Houston, and he performed the second abortion in a hospital. Thinking it might be safer, I awoke from the abortion in my hospital room with the doctor's mouth covering mine with a kiss and his hands on my body. I didn't even realize he was abusing me too. I also had my tubes tied by a tubal ligation so I would never be in this position again. I had lost one child to miscarriage, lost custody of my only living child, aborted two babies, and made it impossible to ever bear another child. I was twenty-five years old and childless for life. This was not because I didn't love children or want to be a mother. It was the result of sin in my life and all the heartbreak sin brought into my broken mothering heart.

The years following the abortions are really a blur. I walked in darkness, and all the time Jesus was with me loving me back to Him. This lifestyle of sin filled me with so much guilt that I thought I could never come back to God. Though desperate for true love, I found none where I was searching.

After marrying Ray, I finally had a man that really loved me, but in my shame and guilt, I couldn't believe it was true love. It seemed impossible to accept that such a good guy could really love me because I had been devalued at such a young age. We had a rocky time for the first three years of our marriage, as I punished him for every man's abuse before we met. My heart was hard, and we were on a collision course with divorce.

Ray knew about my abuse, abortions, and life of sin. What I didn't know was Ray had experienced abortion before we met, and his heart was broken by shame too. I didn't know Ray was struggling to forgive himself and was miserably unsuccessful.

Miraculously, three years after we married and only days before we would have considered divorce as a real option, Ray received Jesus into his heart on October 2, 1981. When he arrived home, and as he told me all about it, "I turned around, bumped into Jesus, and fell into His forgiving arms." For months, all I could do was cry when we started attending church, especially during worship. I was being cleansed in God's loving presence. I had so hardened my heart that I had been unable to cry for years, and now God was tenderizing my heart. It was a precious time of cleansing and renewal.

I accepted God had forgiven me for most of my sin, but I couldn't forgive myself. I thought some of my sin was unforgiveable. That was another lie of the devil.

As I already told you, our life did a complete 180-degree turn about. We immediately began to devour God's Word and worship Him with all our hearts. We loved God for real. As I told you, we served Him fervently for ten years, but there was still a room in our hearts we both refused to look in. I call it the dungeon of my heart, and it was where I buried my deepest, darkest secret sins. All the time all my sin was forgiven, but the heartbreak was not healed until I allowed God to enter that dark room of my heart with His healing touch and amazing grace. It was as if God remodeled that dark dungeon and made it a "son room." It is so beautiful now that it is the room I most want to invite everyone into so they will allow God to shine His light into their darkness. Ray opened his dark room at the same time. We received healing and our marriage was drastically transformed. God restored my calling to teach and preach His Word, but there was more.

Ten years later in a post-abortion healing Bible study, we learned one of the most freeing truths in our lives.

We both learned it was neither biblical nor necessary to forgive ourselves and that God's forgiveness was enough. Our struggle was over.

Great joy returned to our souls!

We heard Christian ministers say to forgive yourself, but now we knew it wasn't necessary or true. We so often hear it today, and hopefully what they really mean is for a child of God to fully accept what Jesus finished on His cross. I pray they will begin to say, "Accept all Jesus did, and let it be enough," instead of giving them a task they cannot perform. For a woman like me and other people who have heinous sins in their past it is a setup for failure to tell us we must forgive ourselves. We don't know how, and we know our sin is more than we can forgive or bear! It is a futile and spiritually destructive exercise in self-righteousness.

So you may ask, freed by God's truth, where did I put all the shame and self-condemnation? I took it to the cross and heard Jesus say, "It is finished!" (John 19:30, NKJV). I let that be enough, for what could I possibly add to what Jesus finished there? Was I to look at Jesus' bloody cross where He hung naked and wounded beyond recognition, shedding holy blood, and think I needed or could possibly do more? God forbid!

No, I accepted all He did as enough and realized so did His Father as He raised Him from the dead and seated Him at His right hand with all authority.

I completely receive and accept what Paul wrote in Romans 8:1, NKJV, "There is therefore now no condemnation for those who are in Christ, who do not walk according to the flesh, but according to the Spirit."

(Walking according to the Spirit simply and profoundly means submitting my will to God's will by the power of the Holy Spirit.)

From this profound truth, I began to live my life as a forgiven child of God instead of a condemned sinner. I have God's righteousness as my new nature. Knowing these truths from God's Word frees me to forgive others. I am set free by God's grace, and I stay free by forgiving others and submitting to God's will in my life.

This great point of grace is major among other graces that govern my life. I am forgiven because Jesus was forsaken, and He finished all He came to do to make that possible!

Acronym for GRACE
G etting
R ewarded
A t
C hrist's
E xpense

- There is nothing you and I can do to earn God's grace.
- There is nothing in us that is good enough to deserve God's grace.
- There is nothing in us good enough to forgive ourselves!
- God is unchangeable, and God is love, so nothing we can do can change His love for us.
- Nothing you will ever do right and nothing you have ever done wrong can make God love you more or less than the day He crucified His Son for you!
- God doesn't love us because we are good; He loves us because He is good!
- God doesn't do love, He is love (1 John 4:8).
- God's amazing grace comes from God's great love.

STAYING FREE

There are two keys to staying free:

Key number 1: Accepting the finished work of the cross to forgive you, realizing

Jesus declared, "It is finished!" and you cannot and need not add anything to it.

Key number 2: Freely forgive everyone, whether they meant to hurt you or not.

I want to be perfectly clear here; again, I am not saying to forgive is to make yourself vulnerable to someone who has abused you. No, forgiveness is a heart-matter and God does not expect you to be hurt over and over again. Forgive from your heart and give those who hurt you to God.

Have you been in sin's prison? Has Jesus set you free? Do you want to go back? Is there any reason why you do not want to stay free indeed? There is liberty in forgiveness when you receive it and give it. It just works that way because God said so and was willing to do so!

And it is my prayer that you never again say, "I know God has forgiven me… but I can't forgive myself!"

Rather, I pray you know and say, "I am completely forgiven and accepted by God in Christ!"

OUR SON

Before Ray and I married, as my son was growing up in his father's home, I would visit or he would visit me. My life was in such chaos that getting ready for a visit from my child would require many drastic changes. Often it required a breakup with someone and moving to a new place. It was quite a production to put on a front for my child that his mother wasn't brokenhearted. I would do anything to make that happen before he came. Parting each time was miserable. I believed I would always only be allowed to visit my child, but my God is a *redeemer* and *restorer*.

Shortly after Ray received Christ and I came running back to Him, our life drastically changed again. While still living in LaGrange, ninety miles from Houston, my son's father brought our son to live with us. I was amazed only weeks after I returned to the Lord my fifteen-year-old son was in my home. He was troubled, and his father finally saw how much he needed his mother.

It was a joy, and at the same time, it was a big challenge. He was determined to quit school and get a job when he came to live with us. So before he arrived, I went to the town square of that little Texas town and found the hardest job I could find. It was a commercial tire store and shop where truckers brought their rigs to be serviced and tires put on their trucks. The location was strategically located next to the only Dairy Queen and across from the high school. I told the shop owner my son was coming and wanted to quit school and I wanted to hopefully show him how hard a job could be without an education. He was a wise man and agreed with my plan and agreed to hire him. This was the tough love my son needed at a time when all I wanted to do was hold him in my arms. I am amazed at the grace God gave me to do what my child needed instead of what I wanted; however, I did hug him a lot. Ray was an amazing daddy to him, and Ray's two sons were great brothers, one two years older and one four years younger.

After he was settled in, we told him he had to get a job if he wasn't going to school. He was excited! I woke before dawn for three mornings, and we went to the local café on the square where all the men went for coffee and breakfast. We were dressed and there by 5:00 a.m. We bought a newspaper, and he had to look through every job ad and choose which jobs he wanted to apply for. We would drive from place to place, and he would apply almost all day and get a "No, you're too young" or "I don't need you." On the third day, I deliberately drove to have lunch at the Dairy Queen. He was thinking he would never get work and looked across the street at the high school with disappointment. As planned, I suggested we go to the tire shop. He was hired as I had been promised and started the next morning at 5:00 a.m.

The first day he came home he was so covered in grease that only the whites of his eyes were visible. He had to undress in the garage. He had been under eighteen-wheelers all day doing lube jobs. His knuckles were bloody, and my heart ached for him, but I couldn't let him know it. I would ask him about his day, cook his and Ray's dinner and then go to my room sick at my stomach and cry over him working so hard. He was too stubborn to say getting a job was a mistake, so I was up at 4:00 a.m. the next day to get him off to work. This lasted a few weeks as he learned that getting a job without an education is not glamorous. Then there were the high school girls he saw walking to Dairy Queen to hang out after school each day. They couldn't see him, but that was the point. He decided he wanted to go back to school but in his former school in Odessa to be with his former friends. He quit his job and was trying to get the grease out from under his fingernails. He worked for a while in the HEB grocery store in LaGrange, and after the summer was over, he was enrolled in his former school back in West Texas. He moved back to his father's home, and we moved back to Houston. On his next visit to Houston, I had the joy of leading him to Jesus one evening in our home.

Before he went back to go to school, we made some great memories. That one Christmas with us in LaGrange is one of them. The guys cut down a tree on the deer lease. It was so huge it covered the car when tied to the top. Ray had tied it back enough to see through part of the windshield. I remember standing on our huge porch laughing as I saw a huge tree with four wheels come slowly up the driveway. We had to cut the top off, and then it took all five of us to hold hands to reach around it. We fell down on the floor laughing and had to go buy all the icicles we could find to finish decorating it. There are other great memories, but that one made up for all the Christmases I suffered without him. We loved each other so much that Christmas as we made Jesus the reason for our celebration.

My precious son still had a wounded heart and went back and forth from our home to his father. He married his childhood sweetheart at seventeen in West Texas, and they had a baby girl at eighteen. Two years later, they had a baby boy. His children are grown now. We had the joy of raising them at different times in their lives. Both of our grandchildren accepted Jesus in our home at a young age and fell in love with Him. We so treasure the memories of those years.

I have to be honest and tell you my relationship with my son is not what the Lord or I want it to be today. The relationship is still wounded after all these years. My greatest desire is that my son will allow his Savior to heal his heart and learn to forgive. I trust my Lord and know he is still working. I'll never give up and neither will Jesus. He is a *redeemer* and *restorer*.

You may be like me and have a big hole in your heart where someone you love should be. The hole in my heart was where my child was missing. It has been over forty-five years since he was taken from me, and I am still trusting God to bring him completely back. I lived my life out of that painful hole until recently when the Lord asked me to let Him heal the last wound. It was Mother's Day 2010 in a Sunday church service. I had skipped church on Mother's Day for years. It was too painful to see mother's honored and celebrate the love of their children when I didn't even get a phone call. Ray would always try to plan a special day for me out of town. He tried so hard to fill the hole but he couldn't. On this particular Mother's Day, God opened my eyes and heart to a truth that had escaped me. What he helped me understand may help you if you are waiting on your child's return.

Jesus told me when my son pulls away from Him, he pulls away from me. Both are due to wounds in his heart I understand all too well. This helped me as I realized it is a spiritual battle and not personal rejection. It is clear to Ray and me now, that because our life is dedicated to healing the brokenhearted with God's love, the devil will try all he can to keep our hearts broken. It isn't going to work. God has filled the hole in my heart with his great love. My greatest desire now is that my child will fully come back to his heavenly Father. I had to give it to God and stop blaming myself, his father, or anyone else. The blame game is futile. I trust my child into God's capable healing hands. As a mother and grandmother, I am patiently waiting on God's restoration.

Another way God has healed my heart is by giving me a mother's love twice. On a different Mother's Day, Jesus showed me my mother loved me as much as she could, she just couldn't. He told me it wasn't me. It was her broken heart. Then I realized He gave me a mother's love when I married young and again when I married Ray. The Lord allowed me to have a very special time with my former mother-in-law on a visit to Odessa after Ray and I married. We talked for the first time about what happened at the Ramada Inn the night they took my son, and she sincerely apologized. We forgave each other, and I saw her countenance change from grief to joy right before my eyes.

Ray's mom was my mother-in-love! We moved Mom in with us after Ray's dad died. She lived six more years, and her love was so healing in my life. It was a great pleasure and honor to be her daughter and care for her as she became bedridden. She was such a lady and loved me unconditionally.

> Looking unto Jesus, the author and finisher of our faith, who for the joy set before Him endured the cross, despising the shame and has sat down at the right hand of the throne of God. (Hebrews 12:2, NKJV)

The word "looking" is a laser focus. I have learned to look to Him to finish all He has planned for my life!

Ray and I will continue to minister to brokenhearted people as we have for over thirty years while trusting the Lord to minister to the ones we love as He finishes what He started in them.

MESSENGERS

I have serious back and neck pain from five auto accidents and multiple resulting surgeries. We were hit from behind in all five accidents, and as the passenger, I was the only one injured. Discouraged by unrelenting physical pain, I talked with my Lord one morning in 2011. I had been thinking for weeks of taking a long break from so much ministry responsibility. Then the morning came when I felt I had to express my true feelings to God in the wee hours before daybreak. I had spent an endless night thinking and finally had to rise and go to my Jesus chair in the corner of my living room. I made a cup of coffee, turned on the floor lamp next to my chair, and picked up my journal and two pens. I reached for a tissue as tears slowly fell on my cheeks.

It is my habit and pleasure to journal my feelings to God. My Lord had taught me to write to Him in black or blue ink but pick up a red pen and then to listen to Him on purpose. I began to do this on January 1, 2000. I bought a red pen and used only that pen to record what God said to me. At the writing of this book, I have "journaled" this way for fourteen years, so you can imagine how many journals

I have filled. That morning it took several minutes before I could see through the tears to write. The tears came slowly at first but had swelled to a waterfall in moments. I wondered why I was crying and struggled to get hold of myself.

I began to write and pour out my heart of discouragement and despair. I asked for God's permission to take a long rest. I felt overwhelmed with a need to stop, to stop everything. I asked if I could give up the two weekly Bible classes I taught at church and postpone the powerful ministry God had given to my husband and me to the brokenhearted women from Houston shelters. I dearly loved to teach, and I knew I could quit, but I didn't want the regrets that can come from quitting. I was asking God for His will but just wanted my own. It was a Gethsemane moment, but I found surrender deafened by the screaming physical pain. I told my Lord I wouldn't tell anyone but Ray until I heard from Him. When I picked up my red pen after asking God for confirmation His answer was not full of drama but pierced my heart. He said, "Confirmation will come soon, trust Me! I know exactly what you need." I told Him okay but would really like to know right then.

At this time, my husband was pulling his weight and mine in the everyday responsibilities of life. I felt guilty as he would do the laundry, the dishes, the shopping, and so much more. On the Friday following my plea for God to release me from my many duties as a minister, I found the determination to dress and accompany my loving husband to Walmart for groceries. The list wasn't long, and I wanted to do something to ease his burden. We walked slowly down the aisles, and I would sit down every place there was seating. On the second and final trip to the produce department, I took a seat at a little table in the deli section. I sat there in self-pity, wondering how in God's name I would make it all the way to the car. Suddenly I found myself on my feet walking toward my husband, looking down at my feet while determined to put one foot in front of the other. I looked up and there, with her shopping basket, was a friend from church standing by and visiting with my husband. She was a friend who could be trusted with your heart.

Before greetings were exchanged, my friend's first words to me were; "Whenever I think of you, I see someone the devil wants to silence." The words were like lightning bolts to my heart. Tears came instantly, and I looked at my husband and said, "There's my confirmation!" We chatted, and I walked away still not completely sure I had received the confirmation I wanted to hear. We shopped a little longer, and I was lagging way behind my husband as he approached the registers. I joined him, but as my legs were buckling from pain, I was desperately looking for anything to sit on. I looked opposite the registers, and there was a bench for two but occupied. I saw the edge of an empty chair behind a partition. There was a woman sitting at a table behind the partition, and I asked if I could use the empty chair for a moment. I pulled it a few inches and sat next to the bench.

As I sat down, I heard a constant deep groan coming from somewhere close. I asked the man sitting closest to me his name, and he said it was Keith. I then asked the woman's name just before realizing the guttural groans were coming from her. Keith said her name was Stacey, she was twenty-seven, and she was autistic and had suffered two strokes. When I asked if she was his wife or his sister, he replied, "No, I am her uncle and watching her while her mother shops." Keith was obviously mentally impaired also and looked amazed someone was talking to him. He told me he was a ticket guy at the stadium, and he helped with Stacey's care a lot. All during the conversation, Stacy groaned loudly as if she was trapped and wanted to speak.

When Ray had finished checking out, he approached us, and I introduced him to Keith and Stacey. He said he would go get the car and meet me at the door. As he walked away, I began to tell Keith of our six-year-old autistic grandson and how God has a plan for every single person. That led to sharing Jesus with both Keith and Stacey. We went to the cross and saw God's great love. Keith said he believed all that when he was a child. We talked further, and I invited them to my church the next Sunday for Easter. Keith knew where the church was and said he might come. I invited Stacy too. I looked up to see Ray coming through the doors with a smile. He knew what I had been doing. He knew his wife would talk to anyone about Jesus who would listen. I said I would see them at church and walked toward my husband with tears running down my cheeks.

When I got to the car and gained enough composure to voice what was flooding my heart, I said to Ray, "God sat me next to a woman, trapped in her body while groaning in effort to speak, while I was groaning about too much speaking! She can only groan, and I groan when I could easily praise."

I will never forget Keith and Stacy. Human beings or angels, I do not know, but I do know God sent me three messengers at Walmart that Friday afternoon to teach the teacher not to give up. One trusted friend and two strangers, all with a message for me that God's callings are irrefutable; His love is constant and His grace is enough. What a faithful God we have! Again, I don't know if Keith and Stacy were angels, for God's Word does tell us we entertain angels when we are unaware (Hebrews 13:2). Whether angels or not, God sat me next to exactly who I needed to hear from, even if what I heard the loudest were only groans from a precious heart.

As I am writing the last chapters of this book in 2013, I sit at my computer so grateful I can serve God with all my heart again. The grocery trip to Walmart was two years ago. The physical pain isn't completely gone yet, but the heartache is healed. It is amazing how a young woman who could not speak taught the teacher gratitude with a groan. God set it all up, but then He always does.

A MAJOR TEST!

I did not know on Easter 2012 that in October I would enter an eight-month affliction that would sorely test me in so many ways. I was diagnosed with a serious condition in my colon. It would be January 2013 before our insurance supplement was in effect, and I could go to a specialist. Ray and I were told it would require major surgery. We knew that was true because my sister had the same condition. The oddest thing about that is it is not hereditary. I had been with her when she was diagnosed and when she had surgery that November. She had complications and was readmitted twice. Five days after her diagnosis in early October, my body shockingly presented the same hideous symptoms. The timing could not have been worse. One week later, I conducted a two-day conference, "Transformed by Grace," and preached six sermons with horrendous symptoms. God's anointing is always more than enough!

My surgery was three months later. All the time I spent with my sister in the hospital, I knew I was facing the same surgery. It wasn't easy, but I believed I would just sail through it all. I was wrong. My surgery ended with a three-month ileostomy bag. My sister's surgery did not require that. I had many complications, and after the reversal of the ileostomy, I was readmitted through the emergency room twice. I had become so disappointed in my surgeon's care that we fired him and hired a different surgeon. He is renowned in Houston, Texas, and my trust elevated. I was admitted to a different hospital, but that was a mistake. My second surgeon reversed the ileostomy and did reconstruction at the site. Post-surgery, my care was turned over to a hospital staff doctor whose treatment was less than standard and without true compassion. Ray was with me through it all, and only the Lord knows what heroics my husband did to care for me. On a Sunday morning in April 2013, at the end of my second readmission, Ray came to take me out of that place! Against the doctor's orders, Ray took me home. I began to progress in healing as soon as he got me home. Looking back, some of what happened to me was truly evil. The people were not evil but the evil one was using them.

My church family surrounded me with prayer and love. It literally saved my life! By this, I realized the responsibility of praying for someone when you can't know what they are facing! It has changed my prayer life. My pastor's wife is really also my pastor. Jana was there with Ray and me so much. She would rub my feet with lotion as she sang sweet Christian songs that encouraged my heart. Ray was so faithful to be there through it all but couldn't possibly be at the hospital all the time. It was when no one was with me that I was mistreated, but my Jesus never left me, and He turned it all around for good (Romans 8:28). I have come through this eight-month trial with a new love for the family of God and for ministry! When no one else seems to care, God's family will love you with His love. Several people received Christ as I shared Him with them in both hospitals, and one nurse's five-year-old son walked for the first time in his life after we prayed. He took ten steps the next morning. When she told me, I didn't remember praying due to the pain and drugs. If we are willing, God will use us even when we are out of it. I know God will use these painful experiences to help many avoid them or get through them by God's grace. I am thankful he chose me for this privilege.

THE RIPPLE EFFECT

We have all tossed a stone into a pond or lake and watched the ripple effect it causes. Our lives can have a similar effect. One Saturday morning in the early 1990s, my husband attended an emergency board meeting at a Crisis Pregnancy Center where we volunteered, and Ray served on the board as I was director of client services. As he left the meeting, the Lord asked him to go to midtown Houston and drive around the Planned Parenthood headquarters and killing center so He could talk to him. He drove around for two hours and came home with shocking news. He sat me down and told me God had asked him to start a Crisis Pregnancy Center and locate it close to Planned Parenthood's main building. That particular Planned Parenthood location was on Fannin Street in Houston, Texas and is a block-long two-story building where they were killing preborn babies six days a week.

It is a long miraculous story how God made the Crisis Pregnancy Center Central possible. Maybe Ray will write a book on that someday. We carried the vision for over two years as God worked on it. God asked Ray to walk away from his successful insurance agency to follow Him full time in ministry. Ray obeyed and my respect for him goes beyond my ability to express with mere words.

Finally, we had a beautiful building separated from Planned Parenthood only by a parking lot fence. This PP was the largest provider of abortion in the State of Texas and third largest in America at that time. Our building faced the main campus of Houston Community College and backed up to PP. It was perfect. God had trained us for this as we served at the other crisis pregnancy center, but it was a huge undertaking as God chose in us, two people who in no way could do it without Him! We opened the doors to clients on March 15, 1997. The first few months were very slow as we got our legs under us. Volunteers came from as far away as Cleveland and La Porte, Texas for training to be peer counselors. We would have sixty to seventy-five trained volunteers to schedule from and were open fifty-four hours a week. We were ready to talk to women about the life of their babies and options other than abortion as well as providing what they needed to be mothers or to place for adoption. The main thing we shared with them was the Gospel of Jesus Christ and how much God loved them.

One day a man walked into the center and offered free signage that made all the difference. The day he installed big red letters on three sides of the building, saying, "Free Pregnancy Tests," the waiting room filled all day long and continued six days a week. In the seven years we directed that Pregnancy Center, we saw thousands of babies saved from abortion, men and women saved from the heartbreak of abortion, and thousands receive Christ as their personal Savior. As ordained ministers we even married some of the couples who chose life for their babies and life with each other. We also walked with men and women through healing from the emotional after-effects of abortion and sexual abuse. Beauty for Ashes Ministries International was birthed there. To God goes all the glory! That pregnancy center is still operating today, and we pray it will as long as needed. The ripple effect of our salvation and restoration from heartbreak has been long and wide, and thousands have been saved and restored by God's grace. Only God can turn the trash of our lives into treasure to be given away.

What we want to bury in shame, God wants to forgive and then resurrect in victory. What we want to deny, God wants to redeem. While we want to give God our very best, He wants our worst, first. There is no shame greater than God's love. He can take the ashes of our lives and bring beauty forth in not only our lives but the ripple effect is unending. For every person God healed through the ministry he birthed from our pain and healing, there may be countless multitudes who received His grace whom we never met. We cannot know how plentiful the fruit will be from the seed God waters year in and year out. It is a profound truth spoken by Robert Schuller, "Man can count the seeds in an apple, but only God can count the number of apples in a seed!"

HOLY BLOOD

You have seen me refer to Christ's blood in this book as *holy* blood. I will give you the reason I do so. I learned about the DNA of human blood in Crisis Pregnancy Center training. There are twenty-three chromosomes in a man's sperm (seed) and twenty-three chromosomes in a woman's ovum (egg). It takes forty-six chromosomes to conceive a human being. When the forty-six chromosomes come together, a life begins, and it is called conception.

An important medical fact to learn about human DNA is human blood comes only from the chromosome in a man's sperm. The woman's ovum contributes absolutely nothing to the blood. So this means your blood came solely from your biological father's sperm.

Why is this important to know? Although Mary was betrothed to Joseph, the miraculous conception of Jesus did not involve a man's sperm. Jesus' mother, Mary, was a virgin when she conceived Jesus, and she gave birth to Jesus as a virgin. She conceived Jesus by the Holy Spirit. At the precise moment Mary surrendered her will to the Word of God, delivered by the angel Gabriel, God the Son was miraculously sent into the womb of this betrothed Jewish virgin teenager. Think of it; the Creator of the universe came to earth as tiny as half a grain of sand in a virgin's womb! This was Almighty God the Son who spoke light into being and the sun came out of His mouth when He said, "Light Be!" He created everything and willingly became the most vulnerable creature as an embryo.

> Then Mary said, "Behold the maidservant of the Lord! Let it be to me according to Your word." And the angel departed from her (Luke 1:38, NKJV).
>
> Read the entire account of this angelic visitation in Luke 1:26–38.

The tiny baby Jesus developed blood in His mother's womb. Whose blood? Joseph had nothing to do with Jesus' conception, so human sperm did not contribute to Jesus' blood. It was Jesus' heavenly Father's holy blood that developed in His tiny veins as he grew in Mary's womb. This was God requiring a price for sin yet providing His own blood to pay the price. When Jesus was beaten and crucified, He willingly shed His Father's blood to pay the price His Father required for sin to be forgiven, and it was holy. Wow, what a plan! We can't top that in any way by our own efforts.

I tell you this to bring to your understanding how powerful forgiveness is and how high a price was paid for your sin to be forgiven! What a marvelous plan and part of that plan is for us to forgive as we are forgiven.

Jesus made a profound statement, and the Apostle John wrote it in his gospel.

> I am the way, the truth and the life. No one comes to the Father except through Me. (John 14:6, NKJV)

Jesus did not say, He is a way, a truth, or a life, but He is *the* way, truth, and life.

You may be reading this book and you know about God but do not have a relationship with Him through Jesus. If you were asked the question, "Who is Jesus to you personally?" would you have to say you do not have an answer to that question? I have just written a lot of truth about God's great sacrificial love for you, so I boldly, and without reservation, invite you to your knees at this very moment. As you physically humble yourself before God, bow your head and heart in humility.

I am asking you right now if there are any reasons to stop you from receiving God's great love and eternal life by making Jesus your personal Savior at this very moment. There is really no reason good enough to keep you from accepting such a great eternal gift, so I will pray a prayer now, and as you read and sincerely pray it with me, meaning every word of it with all your heart, you will be born again in Christ! It is miraculous! Okay, pray this prayer aloud with me and your part is to mean it with all of your heart.

> Dear heavenly Father, I have seen Scriptures say You love me with a great love and sacrificed Your only Son for me. By your written Word, I see that You

sent Jesus to earth to live sinless, to be made to be sin and die, shedding Your holy blood for my sin. I also see that You raised Him from death and seated Him at Your right hand. I believe this. I am a sinner, and I need Your righteousness. I want to exchange my sin nature for your righteousness. I don't know why You want me this much, but I receive You now into my heart and thank You for forgiving me once and for all time. By Your grace, I give You my worst to make room for Your best. Please fill me with Your Holy Spirit. I am Yours, and You are mine!

In Jesus name I pray, Amen.

Scriptures to read confirming this prayer: Romans 3:23, NLJV; Romans 6:23, NKJV; John 3:3 and 16, NKJV; John 10:10, NKJV; Romans 10:8–10, NKJV; 2 Corinthians 5:17 and 21, NKJV.

My new sister or brother in Christ, you now have an eternal love relationship with God! You are joint-heirs with Jesus of this new and better covenant of grace. What you need now is a good Bible-believing church family so you can grow in this new relationship you have with God and His family. Jesus commanded us to be baptized in water and then follow Him (Mark 16:16). It will bless you to do that as soon as possible. Jesus also commands us to forgive as we are forgiven. There is no better moment than now to obey him.

Please pray with me,

Heavenly Father, I am so thankful You have freely forgiven me of all my sin! Your love has set me free. I want to remain free so I will obey You and forgive everyone who has sinned against me.

Name each person as the Holy Spirit brings them to your remembrance and you may write their name or initials here:

_____
_____
_____
_____

Jesus, You are my Lord, and I want to obey You in every way, so please keep me aware of my need to continue to forgive. I love You so much and always will. In Your name Lord Jesus, Amen.

You are in Christ now, so learn all you can from God's Word about what that profound truth means to you. It is also important and powerful to tell others of this new life you have in Christ. I would love to know, and you can contact me on our website, www.lanasanders.com. Now if you do not have a good Bible-believing church already, pray to find one as quick as possible. Holy Spirit will lead you. You need the family of God to help you grow strong in Jesus!

Remember God wants you to be free indeed, so run to Him with everything, and remember to forgive everyone. Also remember that God has completely forgiven you, and it is never necessary to forgive yourself! Accept all that Jesus finished on His cross, and as you obey Him, let that be enough to set you free.

God bless you with everything grace gives you to follow Him wherever He leads.

Continuing in His amazing Grace,
Lana

EPILOGUE

The truth that it is neither biblical nor necessary to forgive yourself may be completely new thought for most of the readers of this book. It is so vitally important to confirm all doctrine and beliefs with God's infallible Word. His Word is truth, and He honors it above His name! The Psalmist David wrote: "For You have magnified Your word above all Your name" Psalm 138:2b, NKJV.

What we believe to be God's truth will greatly influence our lives when we apply it. For this reason, what we believe must be what God says instead of how man interprets what He said or what man's opinion is because it sounds right.

The truth that there is no instruction or admonition in God's Word to forgive self transformed my life drastically as I accepted the finished work of Christ's cross, where I was forever forgiven by a holy God and made to be His very righteousness!

Please do not feel condemned if you have struggled in thinking you must forgive yourself or if you have counseled or taught others to do so. Forgiving self is a popular deception, and the thing about deception is we do not know we are deceived until truth sets us free. I do hope this truth from God's Word sets you free indeed as it set me free from the futile attempt to add to Christ's finished work!

In Christ Jesus,
Lana Sanders

ABOUT THE AUTHOR

Lana is married to Ray Sanders for thirty-five years. They are both ordained ministers of the gospel of Jesus Christ and serve as lay ministers at Lindale Church, under Pastors Randy and Jana Meeks. Ray and Lana have three grown sons and seven grandchildren.

Lana and Ray have been in prolife ministries together for over twenty years, first serving as Crisis Pregnancy Center volunteers, staff, and then board members. Then answering the call of God, together they founded and directed the Crisis Pregnancy Center Central—directly behind Planned Parenthood, seeing thousands of babies and women saved from abortion.

Lana is the founder and director of Beauty for Ashes Ministries International, working with facilitators she has trained. BFAMI has facilitated recovery to hundreds of emotionally wounded women following abortion and sexual abuse. Now through a new model of ministry called Transformed by Grace, BFAMI is reaching women with multiple issues of heartbreak.

She is a published author of prolife resources, training manuals, and a journal series titled *Written in Red*. She writes and teaches Bible studies in her church twice a week and speaks at conferences and retreats across America. She has been the guest speaker on several local Christian radio and television programs and hosted her own Christian television program for one year.

Lana testified before a Texas Senate Committee in May 2003, resulting in the passing of House Bill 15, which gives a woman the right to know the risks of abortion, see the development of a baby in the womb, and mandating a twenty-four-hour waiting period before abortion. She was present when Governor Rick Perry signed the bill into Texas law, January 2004.

The passion of her heart has always been to share the Gospel of Jesus Christ with the lost. Her joy is to see the captives set free from emotional pain, by the teaching of the powerful Word of God, and to see God's children walk in the freedom Christ paid for by His holy blood. She ministers the truth of God's Word so families can heal, making the church stronger, and America mighty again in righteousness. All Lana does for the Lord is Christ-centered and cross-anchored. The finished work of the cross of Christ is the centerpiece of Lana's heart, life, and the anchor of her ministry.

NOTES

1. Hal Lindsey, *The Late Great Planet Earth*, (Grand Rapids: Zonderman, 1970), 134.
2. Charles Swindoll, *The Darkness and the Dawn*, (Plano, Texas: Insight for Living, 1970).
3. William Edwards, *On the Physical Death of Christ*, (Boston, Massachusetts: Journal of American Medicine, 1986).
4. Craig S. Keener, *The IVP Bible Background Commentary on the New Testament*, (Downers Grove, Ill.: Inter Varsity Press, 1993).
5. David W. Wead, *International Standard Bible Encyclopedia, rev. ed.*, (Grand Rapids, Michigan: William B. Erdmans Publishing Co., 1988).

Beauty for Ashes Ministries International

PO Box 7894
Houston, Texas 77270

E-mail: Lana@lanasanders.com
Website: www.lanasanders.com

This book and all products, CDs, DVDs, and resources produced by this ministry are available online. Follow us on Facebook and Twitter and on our website!